Unrepentant

The Story of an Era

By

Gary Lee Wright & Corky Evans

First Edition – September 2012

ISBN
978-1-4602-0056-8 (Hardcover)
978-1-4602-0055-1 (Paperback)
978-1-4602-0057-5 (eBook)

Like most autobiographies, this work is a piece of historical fiction.

It is based on true events.

Except for the chapter written by Corky Evans, and certain persons whose lives are a matter of public record, any resemblance between real people and the characters created herein is a matter of bad luck and coincidence. "Don't Flocculate Me, Mama" first appeared in the Valley Voice and is used with the permission of the publisher, as are brief quotations from the Daily Missoulian.

Published by:

FriesenPress
Suite 300 – 852 Fort Street
Victoria, BC, Canada V8W 1H8

www.friesenpress.com

Distributed to the trade by The Ingram Book Company

For Linda Lea, who I hope will understand,

&

For Fay, the poet in us all

Acknowledgements

The author wishes to thank the staff of the Missoula County Library for placing their resources at his disposal during the preparation of this book, and is grateful to both the Daily Missoulian and the Valley Voice for allowing him to reference information drawn from past issues of their newspapers.

Andrea Kosling and DJ Wright provided invaluable technical and conceptual advice, while Geoff Soch did a commendable job overseeing the editorial process at Friesen Press.

Enough ideas for stories to fill two volumes were suggested by friends in New Denver and the Regional District of Central Kootenay. Some of the best cannot be shared because of the rules of governmental and/or personal privilege; it must be sufficient to say that there is a small village in Canada that owes debts of gratitude to people like John Kettle, John Voykin, and former BC provincial cabinet ministers Corky Evans and Dr. Tom Perry.

Landslide

Slocan Lake 1989

It is the evening of the civic by-election.

The smells of fast food and human bodies filter through the dried window casings of the council chamber and into the public works yard, where they mix with dust, diesel fumes and cedar pollen.

"Council chamber" is a respectful exaggeration for a room barely large enough to hold a table and a dozen old cane-bottomed chairs, and which for the moment is doing double duty as the polling station. It is self-heating in the summer, a sauna when it has been stuffed with voters all day. The poll is closed now, but three people are locked inside, sweating like sheepdogs as they count ballots and munch on the remains of a locally-famous Palmer's All-Meat Vegetarian pizza.

"I have it as 154 to 153," says the elderly town clerk.

"I have 155 to 152," says his secretary.

"Don't you have to agree on at least one number?" asks the scrutineer. His candidate, a popular chimney sweep, seems to be on the short end of both sticks.

"What do we do now?" asks the clerk. If it was solely left to him, what he would do now would be to open some of the plastic bottles from the mini-bar he keeps hidden in the lower desk drawer of his office.

"We do a recount," says the secretary, who knows exactly what her boss is thinking.

The ballots are once more put into a big pile. The clerk takes the top one, checks it and calls out the name of the candidate who has been marked. He passes it to the secretary and the scrutineer for confirmation before moving on to the next.

It is a crying shame that the mayor's doctor told His Worship to resign before he had a heart attack, the clerk thinks as he counts. Ever since he's been here, the mayors have resigned or died in office before their term was up. Is the job that hard?

He voted for the chimney sweep himself, and is secretly hoping for a dead heat so that as Chief Elections Officer he can vote again to break the tie. That is the law. But he won't cheat. As usual, his secretary got it right the first time: 155 to 152. He purses his lips.

"Okay, the hippie wins. Lord have mercy."

Missoula

To live outside the law, you must be honest.

Bob Dylan

When they said, "Repent! Repent!"
I wondered what they meant.

Leonard Cohen

Snowballs

Quench not the Spirit.
Despise not prophesyings.
Prove all things; hold fast that which is good.

I Thessalonians 5:19-21

Missoula 1966

Nighttime, and more snow was falling on the Missoula campus. Absent-mindedly strumming my guitar, I sat at the desk in my dorm room and wondered what to do about New England Puritans, the Reverend Jonathan Edwards (long deceased) and Dr. John Van de Wetering, my history professor – who was still very much alive. Snow muffled the usual sounds of students running around outside and music pumping from the Union.

I was in a pickle because earlier in the day I told the professor that my senior American History seminar paper on the famous Reverend Edwards would expose that worthy as a cant-ridden, marginally-socialized schizophrenic. Van de Wetering smiled and confided: his own doctoral dissertation had been on Edwards – his philosophical brilliance and his lasting influence on national religious thought, why there might be some academic risk in attacking an American icon, that he was considering me for the plum job of his undergraduate teaching assistant.

Intellectual integrity? Moral compromise? Did I have the former? Would I make the latter? Is "intellectual integrity" in an ambitious teenager nothing more than egotistical persistence in one's own shallow reasoning? Does "moral compromise" apply to trivialities, especially if it may result in future influence over issues of greater moral consequence? And a job as teaching assistant? At least I got to think about pickles in my own room. That year, only my second in college, I was the Residential Assistant for Craig Hall, one of the men's dormitories. An RA got his own room. Everyone else bunked, discovered the joys of underage drinking and sometimes studied four-to-a-room.

The phone rang. It was the Head Resident, an upperclassman who got a paycheck as well as room and board for riding herd on the whole testosterone-riddled hall. He said that Chicken Little had called to tell him to stop the riot Craig boys were causing at one of the women's dorms. Chicken Little was our nickname for the Dean of Men. A job of head residents and their assistants was to help the dean make sure the university would still be there each morning after the two retired town cops, who constituted the campus police force, went home to nap at 5 p.m.

"He's pretty jumpy after last night," said the HR. "Would you deal with it? I'm in my pajamas. Call me back." The night before, city police and even the fire department had been summoned to Brantley Hall to break up a gang of underclassmen who were pelting the building with snowballs after the girls cloistered there had challenged them to a snowball fight. Brassieres and panties had been tauntingly waved from the top floor. Windows had been broken and the *Daily Missoulian* reported that the housemother's nerves were shattered. Police Officer Drinville got swarmed by the crowd when he tried to arrest one kid. The newspaper said that the cruiser was "rocked." There had been "a lot of swearing" and eventually three students were hauled off to jail. One of them was the son of an influential former mayor of Billings. The dean had caught holy hell from University President Robert Johns for letting things get out of hand.

I checked the hallways at Craig. They *were* quieter than normal, with no soap fights or Frisbee games in the corridors. I went outside into the cold. In the seconds before my glasses steamed over, then frosted and left me blinder than a blinkered mule, I saw our guys. For a second night they were cheerfully throwing snowballs at beleaguered Brantley. Its windows were full of girls just as cheerfully waving bras and squealing if a snowball hit them. It had been a long winter. Teenagers in heat. There I was, a short kid with iced-over glasses, a year younger than my classmates. My voice was still breaking. Intimidating physical presence was not a card that had been dealt me in the Great Hand of Life, but the dean had his shorts in a knot. It was my duty to do something.

★★★

I can't remember ever trying to be crazy or unconventional.

I was a normal white kid with a teenager's typical interest in Motown and sousaphone music, girls, 17th-century western secular and ecclesiastical history, and sports.

The trouble, if you want to call it that, began in Salt Lake City, Utah, when my parents conceived me as a lustful by-product of watching Tom Mix perform horse and lariat tricks at a theatre. They were newlyweds from Montana and wanted to see big city lights on their honeymoon. You have to be a Mormon or be from Montana or North Dakota to truly appreciate Salt Lake City. Tom Mix was a famous Hollywood cowboy who could still draw a crowd in the Wasatch. My mother could see him using a ladder to mount his horse in one of the wings offstage. I am certain it was an exciting show. Nine months later, back along the Yellowstone River in Livingston, I was born near-sighted in an old whorehouse that the madam had converted to a maternity hospital when she and her girls hit their fifties.

My father, Kenneth Earl, was a career army Master Sergeant who turned down Officers' Candidate School. He said that most military officers are dangerous morons. He accurately defined a moron as someone slightly smarter than an idiot, who can be trained to both issue and comply with simple directions.

He saw the world with jaundiced eyes, but believed in neon and loved the way its electrified particles lit the night.

He grew up during the Roaring Twenties and Great Depression, wrangling horses and going hungry on the family dude ranch in the Boulder River Canyon. The U.S. army rejected him on medical grounds when he volunteered for duty in 1941, then turned around and drafted him in 1942. Given his choice of service branches, he opted for the cavalry because he could shoe horses and drive heavy equipment. I guess that's why he was made a drill instructor, then a bacteriologist in the medical corps. He developed a chemical stain – named after him – that identifies one of the 10,000 wretched tropical diseases awaiting visitors to Southeast Asia.

My mother, Doris Olinger, was raised on a neighbouring ranch that went through even harder times in the 30s. Being the youngest of five floursack sisters made "Doodie" socially adept, with a penchant as an adult for shoplifting clothes and competing for the affections of her daughter's boyfriends.

My sister, Fay, was born in 1949. She was named after Dad's mom, who died of milk fever when Dad was very young. My grandma Hazel Wright – as I knew her – was really my grandma Fay's sister. Hazel's husband had also died early, leaving her with a child. In the days before government social programs, it made practical sense for widowed in-laws to marry. Unlike the Olingers, the Wrights were eminently practical.

I went to a lot of army-base grade schools. At Fort Sam Houston, Texas, the pupils started every day singing "The Eyes of Texas Are upon You," then "The Star-spangled Banner," then recited the Lord's Prayer. I remember thinking that there sure are a lot of people seeking our allegiance. Dad would have said that is because there are a lot of hustlers looking for self-affirmation and other people's money.

Mom delivered my brother, Ken E., while Dad was stationed at the Presidio of San Francisco in 1954. Ken E. was his full name. Not Kenneth Earl Junior or Clarence Kenneth Earl or Bubba. Ken E., period. Dad said that names of more than four letters were too long, tedious to enter on official forms, so my brother spent his whole life having to explain at length on official forms that his legal name *was* Ken E., period.

Dad retired from the military and went to work at a private laboratory in Olympia, Washington. As a high-school student in nearby Lacey, I got elected president of the Thurston County Youth for Goldwater in 1964. Barry Goldwater was the Republican candidate for U.S. president that year. The Wrights had been Republican since the days of Abe Lincoln and great-great grandpa Charles of the Iowa Volunteer Cavalry. It had nothing to do with philosophy or good sense; it was a matter of clan identity. Grandpa Earl thought big businessmen were all crooks, brought a socialist community-owned telephone system to the Boulder Canyon and voted Republican his whole life.

Goldwater was called a "war hawk" and extremist by the Democrats. Maybe he was. We'll never know because he lost the election to Lyndon Johnson, who promptly expanded the scale of the war in Vietnam. Goldwater – or one of his speechwriters – said,

Extremism in the defense of liberty is no vice, and moderation in the pursuit of justice is no virtue.

I loved that line. Still do.

I quote it to the resigned annoyance of my friends all the time. I would learn that the Republicans and I had different definitions of liberty and justice, but they are principles I took to heart – with then unexpected repercussions.

The week after high-school graduation, my girlfriend, Frankie, told me it was time to propose to her. I did. She accepted, then bought an engagement ring for me to give her. We were both 17 and had been together since junior high. I practically lived at her place. She had her own room and shower across the carport from the main house. Whenever I was there, her mother always knocked on the door before coming in. Frankie's younger sister didn't. Sisters.

Frankie enrolled in the computer technology program at Olympia's newly opened Evergreen Community College. She wanted to be a computer programmer, said to be the Job of the Future. I wanted to be a lawyer in Big Timber, Montana, maybe a mayor or state representative someday. Big Timber is where the Boulder splashes into the Yellowstone. My maternal grandparents, Ross and Dorothy, had lived there in a cabin after losing the Seventy Acres ranch, which followed Ross' loss of the Whispering Pines ranch, which followed his fire sale of the potato farm in what is now downtown Billings. Big Timber is not to blame for me wanting to make it my hometown. I headed for there and the Boulder every chance I had, even if the rest of the family couldn't. Home life was unpleasantly tense: Dad eventually divorced Mom.

The University of Montana in Missoula had a good law school. I decided to get an undergraduate degree in economics and political science, be the first Wright to attend college. Frankie said she would help pay my way when she finished at Evergreen. Military service might or might not come later. Scholarship students like me didn't get drafted. If I did, so be it. From almost everything I'd been told, the war in Vietnam was a righteous one.

Almost everything. There were rumours from foreign and therefore unreliable sources that, as far back as WWII, the U.S. had promised Ho Chi Minh and the Vietnamese people free and open elections within a united country as soon as they helped us beat their brutal Japanese invaders. Unfortunately Ho was a communist and our government explained that it was impossible to have free and open elections with communists on the ballot because those people can't be trusted to keep their word. Most Americans agreed. Sharing and defending popular though unjustifiable political beliefs has always made it easier to get a job as a teacher, trucker, policeman or journalist in America.

Almost everything. I had a cousin, a Green Beret, who started parachuting into North Vietnam in '62 to try and raise a revolt against the commies. He got promoted to sergeant a couple of times. His men loved him, especially the day he shoved his squad's first and only black man out of a helicopter two thousand feet over the jungle, then emptied a clip of M16 rounds in his general direction as the soldier frantically searched for his ripcord. "You should have seen him," he said. "The jigaboo's eyes were as big as saucers! He transferred back to the grunts (infantry) as soon as he got out of the trees!" My cousin kept getting busted back to corporal, once as punishment for shooting up a village of "friendlies" during a drinking binge. That made me wonder what you had to do to get busted back to a private. He didn't trust airplanes; insisted on packing his own 'chute onto commercial flights. God bless America and all those who serve as her ambassadors.

***

Where was I? Oh, yeah. It was my duty to do something.

I groped my way back into Craig Hall and called Matthew, Mark, Luke and Sidney out of their rooms. They were known as the Apostles. They were all honour students. I knew they would be awake and studying. And they were tall. Matt had been an all-state tight end on Butte's high-school football squad. The only people wild enough to mess with big men from Butte were those from neighbouring Anaconda, where the lead and mercury levels from the smelter made everybody bug-eyed, short-lived and mad as hatters. Mark was from Anaconda.

"Guys, I need your help."

So it was me who talked them into going outside that night to chivvy the young stallions back into the corral. I didn't bother going back outside with them; they could handle the situation.

Within half an hour everyone had settled down. I called the HR and told him all was well. He said that was good because he'd heard that Chicken Little had shown up in person to help quell the hijinks.

In the morning the dean expelled the Apostles.

I skipped class for the first time in my life, running over to Main Hall to say that a terrible mistake had been made. The dean sat squat and solid behind his mahogany desk. "I was there," he said. "Didn't see you. I saw them. Ringleading."

I told my friends not to worry. Whatever it might take to do so, I'd get them readmitted.

I appealed the expulsions to the faculty court that dealt with such things. Its members didn't even allow me to testify on my friends' behalf. They upheld the dean. I was stunned. When I asked the Student Union Council for help, the "Leaders of Tomorrow" declined to protest the faculty's decision because doing so would surely hurt their academic careers. They were right, of course. Leaders are smart like that.

That's when Mark took a .38 Special and shot himself. A permanently debilitating but non-fatal stomach wound. The last I saw of him, he was being yarded away in an ambulance.

Sidney's parents flew out from Chicago to bring their boy home. Luke's did the same. Matt was emotionally broken; I think he was in the psych ward at Warm Springs for a while. I was in a car that passed him hitchhiking alongside the highway near Butte a year later. I had a ride. He didn't.

The university fired me as an RA for speaking to the Student Union against my employer. I cut more classes while getting the local news outlets involved in the story. They jumped on it; it made good copy. Remember, *moderation in the pursuit of justice is no virtue.* But I didn't know much about organizing a real protest.

Joe Kerkvliet did.

Joe had spent time in Alabama as a Civil Rights worker. That was rare for a Rocky Mountain pre-law student. He'd seen some heavy stuff, and he'd seen the power people can have for good or evil when they're in lockstep. He knew how to escalate a situation. We had shared a lot of classes together, arguing about almost everything. I think he believed in the perfectibility of Man. I didn't, and still don't. When he offered to organize a protest march to reinstate the Apostles, I said sure, and worked with him to make it happen.

The march was one of Joe's triumphs. Two thousand people converged on Main Hall and held a rally on its moderately-imposing granite steps. The next day President Johns announced that the Apostles could come back to school, that charges had also been dropped against the mayor's son and his buddies. Johns was doing his best to dig his way out of this mess.

Then it was time for a few people to pay the piper.

Chicken Little was quietly given an early retirement package. Politically adept though he was, within a year Robert Johns was fired by the university's trustees for being a weak-kneed liberal.

That was too late to save the place from its students, who were finding their voice. By then the football team had started smoking marijuana and winning games; the forestry students had succeeded in getting their mascot – a stuffed moosehead – elected Campus Queen; the girl who as Miss Montana would get tossed out of the 1968 or '69 Miss America Pageant for giving the country yet another gloved Solidarity Fist had started class as a freshman.

I don't know why Joe quit, but I had been encouraged to leave school by my failing mid-term grades. My test scores were fine; non-attendance at classes and public denigration of authority were the unforgivable insults. To my mind only the biology department kept its head during the snowball furor. Although its faculty accused me of stealing midterm tests from one of the fraternities when I scored 99.5% on mine (Huh? They knew the fraternities had them?), they gave me my grade when I sailed through a specially-convened review panel's oral exam with 98%.

Dropping out of college was going to break my dad's heart, I figured. He had worked hard to get me there, and paid my basic tuition. He had so proudly driven me to Missoula for registration the year before. It was also going to foul up Frankie's plans for our future. She would be mad and think I'd lost my marbles for being quixotic. So for weeks I simply didn't tell anybody back home what was happening to me. There are many ways to cut the ties that bind.

The Apostles' reputations had been upheld by a different breed of people than those with whom I'd grown up: artists with no special respect for societal norms and political activists bent on changing them. The Powers That Be depend upon most of us acting rationally in the interests of self-preservation and self-aggrandizement. These people couldn't act in rational self-interest if they tried. They were screwy. They were hopeless agents of change. Some of them were brilliant. Some were real sick puppies. They deserved, but did not receive, the respect Arab cultures once gave to whirling dervishes. They believed that the Vietnam War was illegal (they were right, only Congress can declare war – and it never did, and never does anymore), immoral and (not that it mattered to them) unwinnable. With a new-found and unflattering personal perspective on our country's conservative elite, I could see why they felt that way. In Missoula a gang of them lived on East Front Street, right across the Clark Fork River from the university. I fell in love with them all. It made sense to rent a cellar room on East Front and live in the midst of such spiritual magic.

The cellar's owner was an old man who gave me cheap rent; said he liked college kids. I guess he did. With his pecker hanging out, he broke into my room every night, trying to get into bed with me. I told him I'd turned down an English prof who offered to pay my way through school if I'd be his boyfriend, but the guy was tediously persistent. It's funny how our needs can make us think we are more attractive to others than we really are. After a couple of spiritually magical weeks without sleep I moved into the garret of a big house full of crazies.

Like thousands of other collegiate, white, middle-class Americans, we were bonded by a sincere desire to promote both world peace and free love – in no particular order. I decided that I needed to liberate myself before I could truly help others. I got drunk for the first time…remember standing under a trillion-volt electrical tower telling Lynn Baker that I would catch him if he jumped from the top. It wasn't a dare; he was already standing up there swigging beer. I was certain I could break his fall. Next thing I knew he was pulling me by the heels out of Rattlesnake Creek, which had somehow grabbed my head and was trying to drown me.

Another time I set a personal record by drinking a fifth of vodka in an evening. I felt amazingly coherent and talkative until the amphetamines wore off. I regained consciousness early in the morning, lying on the centreline of East Front by the little WPA bridge that was thrown across the Rattlesnake in the 30s. Snow was off the street. I hadn't frozen to death. Buds were on the elm trees. Spring was on the way. Life was good. I had learned something: it is wise to keep a constant high amphetamine level in your bloodstream when you are drinking.

By 1966 the US had deployed hundreds of thousands of unmotivated troops across South Vietnam. Other hundreds of thousands of Americans publicly protested. One of those protest marches was in Missoula. Nobody got killed, but it was bloody and peculiarly Montanan: organized by Joe Kerkvliet and the Federal Bureau of Investigation, with most of the injuries being suffered by the parade's hecklers rather than the demonstrators. Let me explain.

FBI Director J. Edgar Hoover sent undercover agents to infiltrate all the anti-war groups springing up across the country. He suspected them of harbouring communists and provocateurs. We got our first fed when Joe set up a committee to plan a protest march. Posing as a grad student in political science, a 35 year-old man with a crewcut started showing up at our meetings. He would go on long rants about what a great place the Soviet Union was and how he could help us make bombs to blow up jeeps at Fort Missoula, the little army reserve post on the edge of town. Joe and I knew all the poli-sci grad students; hell, we were reviewing most of their Master's theses for profs who had more important things to do. Actually, I think they did this as a way to give us money for food, but that's another story. At any rate none of us thought the Soviet Union had a good government, and we didn't think that attacking Fort Missoula would significantly raise the level of national dialog.

We put him on our Executive Committee. What some people won't do for a dollar. Joe would be the Parade Marshal; the FBI dude would be Vice Marshal (it was a private joke). I would be a monitor, walking up and down the parade line between the demonstrators and the crowd, keeping the peace and helping anybody who got injured as we marched from campus to the Higgins Street bridge, then across the river to the post office downtown. We expected trouble. Joe had us practice collapsing into the non-violent fetal position. I couldn't help but ask if there was a violent fetal position.

Less than a hundred people were in that march, but it caused a big buzz across the state. Joe, our J. Edgar clone, and the East Front Gang led the way carrying homemade placards. One of the Gang – Jay Rummel, who later became a well-known sculptor, potter and woodcut artist – was worried about keeping his temper in check if anybody threw stuff at him. "Are you sure you want me in front?" he asked. "I'm no pacifist. I just think the war sucks." His friend Enoch Barnes felt the same. I told them to take some Valium and see if that helped. We all got free Valium from the psychology students, who seemed to get lifetime prescriptions for the drug when they declared their major.

The East Front bunch was followed by some college kids, old profs like septuagenarian Cynthia Schuster and young ones like 28 year-old Barclay Kuhn. I had taken courses in logic and introductory philosophy from Dr. Schuster. She had given me high marks in both courses, but told me to never register for another class from her. "You believe that philosophy is illogical," she had said. "It is. So is everything else. And you believe that most philosophers are *poseurs*. They are, yet their intentions are lofty. You're not meant to be a philosopher. Do something else. You give me migraines." Barclay was a Quaker who taught left-wing political theory. I had loved his courses, not least because he had once caught me ghostwriting a research paper as a lark for another student. He had pencilled an "A" grade onto the ghostwritten one and a lowly "B" onto my own, with a note that read *I like the one you faked for ___ better.* He and his attractive wife, Elsie, pulled their two children in a little red wagon, followed by a carful of standard FBI agents taking lots of pictures of Elsie through their windshield. In local parlance, I started the parade riding "drag" at the rear of the line. Some policemen directed traffic. That was it.

Along South Higgins bystanders alternately cheered and jeered us as if they were at a ballgame until we got to the bridge and faced the gauntlet of Missoulians who didn't go to college and who didn't think highly of the way we were ruining their war morale. The first eggs were lobbed, then tomatoes and balloons full of water. North of the bridge, people began spitting and throwing rocks at us.

Looking up the line, I saw our agent wince a couple of times as he got hit. Served him right. The guy should have been out there arresting people for assault instead of pretending to be a hippie and fomenting attacks on our military depots.

A stone clipped the head of one of Barclay and Elsie's kids, knocking it backwards on its little red wagon. The FBI rolled film. Before I could get to the baby, Elsie had picked it up, kissed away the blood, and tried to bury it between her breasts. I'll never forget the look she gave me when I jogged up and asked her if everything was alright.

I kept between Elsie and the crowd until Barclay shouldered me away. I was in his rightful place. He now carried their other child tucked inside his sport coat against his chest. More rocks rattled against the empty wagon.

I was mad; went to the FBI agents in their sedan and asked them to do something to protect the marchers. They said they were only there to observe and report. An egg somebody had thrown at me missed and hit one of them instead. The crowd laughed. It was an instant lesson about crowds. The agents quickly rolled up their windows, cameras still running. I hopped onto the car's hood, thinking, *Watch this, morons.* In less than a minute the vehicle was splattered with tomatoes and egg yolks, windows and chassis chipped by rocks. Let the feds experience *that* on video replay. Nothing hit me. Nothing. It was weird. I went back to walking up and down the rear of the protest line.

The epithets and pelting lasted until we got to the post office, where contrary-minded citizens charged the head of the parade to keep Joe from giving his planned anti-war speech through one of the squealing battery-powered bullhorns everybody used back then. The attack was perhaps a mistake on their part. There are still pictures at the county library from the *Daily Missoulian* showing Jay Rummel and Enoch Barnes and the East Front Gang calmly clubbing them with peace signs, clearing a path for Joe to gain his vantage point on the post office steps. To their credit, the city cops did no more to prevent this than they had done to stop anything that day. Montana.

Later some of us went to Enoch's to celebrate. He and his girlfriend disappeared into the bedroom to burn each other with lit cigarettes and then ball. They were into that kind of thing. The rest of us shared some joints and beer. Rummel pulled his long, greasy black hair in embarrassment, apologizing for "goin' Injun" on the counterdemonstrators. Except for Joe, we all laughed and told him he'd done fine – after all, he was part Crow or Blackfoot and only acting naturally. Joe said we had shown no commitment to pacifism or route discipline.

Half a dozen men who had not so happily been drinking elsewhere kicked in the front door and poured into the living room. One of them waved a hunting knife. Enoch hopped out of the bedroom, pulling up his shorts.

"Get out of my house," he said.

The guy with the knife said, "Not until we beat the hell out of you all."

Rummel broke the neck off his beer bottle and got ready for a fight. Even Marybeth Kittredge looked scared, and she wasn't afraid of much. I remember thinking that this might be a good time for me to show a greater commitment to pacifism, fall down, curl up and hope nobody killed me.

Others in the room besides me must have felt the atmosphere was getting too dangerous. When Joe started lecturing everybody on America's sad role in Vietnam, Marybeth told him to be quiet. The guy with the knife made a move towards Joe, but before Rummel could intervene the guy's friends pulled their leader back. Even young bucks can sometimes recognize a precipice when they see it. Enoch challenged the guy to arm wrestle, the loser and all his friends were to leave the house. Everybody agreed. This sounds stupid as hell, but I'm telling the truth here. Enoch's girlfriend came out of the bedroom to watch. Angry in jockey shorts, he was strong, built like a fireplug. A small fireplug. The rowdy was taller, heavier, just as strong, and took him down after a struggle. Strange though it would be, from my readings of the classics I expected to follow my defeated champion out into the street, leaving the belching victors in possession of the house and its beer fridge. We all stood around awkwardly while Enoch went into the bedroom to get dressed. He returned in blue jeans, carrying a shotgun which he levelled at the rowdy's belly. You could see that – despite his name – Enoch was more of a modernist than a classicist.

"Get out of my house," he said. "Everybody."

We all did. It is a sad fact of life that in the short run words seem to carry more weight when backed by preponderant firepower.

I hitched a ride to Lacey. It was time to tell my family and Frankie face to face about my changed circumstances. Mom cried. Dad was disgusted. Fay said she was proud of me. Ken, now 12 years old, showed me how – for reasons unknown – he was teaching himself to play guitar using only his thumbs. Frankie handed me back the diamond ring she had bought for herself. If you think that was sad, you're right. She thought I'd gone nuts; didn't want to talk at all. It's a good thing I wasn't seeking empathy, but in truth I hadn't exactly confided in her and looked to her for support and advice as she had every right to expect from her future husband. I only stayed a day.

Back in Missoula, that wonderful pocket of sawmill fumes and lilacs in the mountains, I kicked around the dirt alleys for a few nights, making dogs bark while I mused on first love, love lost, chapters of life closed forever, new chapters starting, and callow true stuff like that. I had no regrets and looked forward to whatever strange twists of fate the future held in store. That's youth for you. I was going to keep Frankie's ring all my life; ran out of grocery money and hocked it for forty dollars at a pawnbroker's.

Corky's Book

His partner Helen is out of town for the Christmas holidays. The five-acre nursery is wrapped in burlap and buried under snow until spring, so former provincial cabinet minister Conrad Evans has a few days on his hands to answer a question from his friend, the mayor of New Denver.

"How in the world did we end up in these mountains, Corky?"

He thinks, how does anyone end up anywhere? Pure and inevitable circumstance. He sweeps the breadcrumbs off the kitchen table – good thing Helen isn't here to watch – and sets up the laptop to write a reply.

Oakland 1966

I don't remember what year it was when it all started to fall apart. Sometime around 1964 or '66 or '68. It was falling apart for a long time.

I first heard about the Vietnam war from my brother Lynden. I lived in Arizona and he lived in Berkeley, California. Arizona was such a militantly conservative place that its high school teachers had to pass out parental release forms to teach history if it involved mentioning the Soviet Union or discussing any political system besides our own. I lived in Tucson, where the air force had a huge airbase. Howard Hughes had one there, too, flying a private air force under contract to the CIA and the U.S. armed services to do the dirty or secret jobs they couldn't do.

I was an American 16 year-old kid. Military service was assumed. If I didn't make my bed, my mother would say, "I give up on you. The army will have to straighten you out." My stepbrothers and I owned guns and played in the desert. The idea of political action against the interests of the United States was as foreign to me as learning to speak another language: I knew it was possible, but it had nothing to do with my life. Then Lynden, one of my brothers, wrote to me saying that he was going to participate in a march against the war in Vietnam.

I didn't, of course, tell anybody. This was an embarrassing thing, like having your brother turn out to be gay or a criminal. I didn't know what to think.

I was in a play in my high school drama program, and I did well. The drama teacher wrote to my parents and thanked them for my participation in the production. Emmerson, my stepfather, who wasn't used to getting letters from teachers praising his kids, thought he would set an example for the five of us at home. He brought the letter to the dinner table, read it out and said, "We need to reward success, so I am going to let Corky pick whatever special favor he desires, and – within reason – I'll give it to him."

I said I wanted to borrow his Chevrolet convertible for the weekend, and take a friend to Flagstaff to check out the college there. He agreed because it sounded like a good, reasonable idea leading to a higher education. The friend wasn't a guy, she was a pretty girl whose dad flew planes in Vietnam for Howard Hughes. I don't remember if I told Emmerson that his Chevy was being used for me to spend the weekend with Laura. A week or two later she and I were driving across the desert at night, listening to the radio and drinking coffee from a thermos when the news came on and said that a demonstration against the war had taken place in Berkeley, California. This unheard-of event turned out okay, the announcer hastened to add, because the Hells Angels had ridden into the march and broken it up.

That was when I realized that Laura and I were probably not going to be any more to each other than kids on a weekend in Flagstaff. I was scared for my brother; she was cheering for the Angels. I said nothing, but started to doubt and wonder. Doubt and wonder changed everything.

Later that year one of my friends invited me into his room to listen to something. He was excited and secretive, like he had something to show me that was illicit or illegal. It turned out to be a record by some guy named Bob Dylan, and it added music and language to the adolescent doubt and wonder in my head. It wasn't information that changed America; it was poetry.

Two years later, give or take a year or so, I was living in Oakland with my family. By then the Vietnam war had become "legal," and the real air force had replaced the contracted one. We had a draft, and I had a draft number. Nothing made any sense. I had no trouble with the idea of "service." Everyone in my father's generation had "served." My dad enlisted for WWII and then re-enlisted for Korea. My dad's best friend, the man who I had lived with in the family basement for a summer, had been a decorated war hero. His name was John Motlow, and he blew his brains out in our garage.

I remember the only time John Motlow talked to me about war. It was during that summer. I was in love with a girl named Cindy Everest, whose father was a test pilot and general. She had just moved from Tucson to Las Vegas so her dad could take charge of the Strategic Air Command base there, the one where they had bombers with nuclear weapons in the sky 365 days a year.

I missed Cindy and admired her dad. John and I were talking one night when my family was gone from the house, and he said, in the way that you do to young people, "So, Corky, what do you want to do when you finish school?"

"I'd like to join the air force and learn to become a pilot," I said without the slightest hesitation.

John's face lost all its warmth.

"Oh, that's a good idea," he said coldly. "Then you could kill people from 20,000 feet, and you wouldn't even have to watch them die."

He committed suicide soon afterwards, leaving his words to echo like thunder in my mind.

Eventually I resolved to apply to serve in the military as a non-combatant, a conscientious objector. I got all kinds of people to say I was a good person as I filled in forms to get ready for a meeting with my draft board. My godfather had been a war hero in WWII, and was now a dean at the University of California, so I asked him for a letter of support. Writing that letter stressed him a lot. He wrote it under protest and out of love. It tested his sense of his religion and his notion of himself as an American, and his faith in me and in his country. But he wrote it. The draft board decided that I was more of a communist than a Christian, and denied the application.

By then, opposition to the war had reached "critical mass," and the Hells Angels could no longer break up the demonstrations because people everywhere were taking to the streets in the tens of thousands.

Somebody planned a big day of national protest for what I think might have been October of 1966.

Lynden had dropped out of college and had long hair and dressed in a serape. He looked like Clint Eastwood gone counter-culture. He decided to ride on a bus to the Pentagon for this day of protest. The plan of the people on the bus was to travel across the United States learning about the "military-industrial complex" by visiting its bases, factories and transportation systems: in other words, to study war from the vantage point of its place of origin, from those who live and profit from it, rather than from its place of action.

His girlfriend, Janie, and I went to see him off on the bus. We both felt weird. Lynden was getting stranger and stranger, and we knew him less and less. This venture was scary and quixotic. He was going to visit America where it lived. He was going to end up at the home of the beast, the Pentagon, where nobody I knew had ever gone.

He left sane.

I never saw him sane again.

Lynden wrote to me as the bus moved east. He wrote about the places he visited; the reactions of the people he met. His words became jumbled and chaotic. He ceased making sense. By the end, he wrote only in images. Probably Janie was getting the same kind of correspondence. Somewhere in that time she must have given up on him. I don't think I ever saw her again.

My younger stepbrother Andy said that he was going to take part in the national day of protest. I was scared. I had been to some of the preparatory demonstrations, and believed that regular people were being drawn into something that was going to be awful. Frankly, I didn't want to go, but my little brother sort of shamed me into it by his resolve. He never asked me to go.

On the eve of the protest, my father came home from work freaked out. I think he might have been crying. He worked as a public defender at the courthouse. The police garage was across the street, and he had seen a big machine that looked like a tank. He said the police called it "Mother," and had brought it in for crowd control. He was frightened and tried to talk us into staying out of trouble.

"Don't worry, Dad," said Andy. "Joan Baez will be there." Andy was a pacifist and had heard there would be a special place for people who wanted to participate in non-violent demonstration with Joan Baez. Surely, nothing would happen to pacifists in her company.

I said I would go with Andy; we would look after each other and be okay. The protest seemed to be organized down to the smallest detail. People who wanted to participate in non-violent action were told to go to a church in Oakland for further instructions. Everyone else would spend the night at an event in Berkeley, then march to the Oakland induction centre in the pre-dawn.

Andy and I spent the night in the church basement with a few dozen other people. When they learned that Andy had a motorcycle, he was asked to be a messenger for the various groups marching through Oakland. He agreed and left to get his bike. That was the end of us looking after each other. I didn't see him again until he got out of Santa Rita prison a week or two later.

We marched in the morning. We walked through Oakland's toughest bar district, past the rundown hotels that provide single housing to men who have little money. In a romanticized version of political activity these citizens would have supported the demonstrators; in reality they lined the street and yelled insults at us. It was terrifying. None of us in the parade said a word for fear of starting a confrontation before the one we had come to provoke. I was nineteen or twenty years old; didn't have a clue about what I was doing, how to do it, or what the consequences would be. In my naiveté, in my heart, I thought we were going to sit in the street and then go home to our comfortable lives.

Weeks later I went to a rally over a different issue in the black community. A speaker there referred to the demonstration at the induction centre, and said that the funniest thing about it – for him – had been seeing all these thousands of white kids sitting in the street, singing songs in the dark and believing that everything was going to be fine because it always had been fine – for them – while the combined police forces of all the communities in central California waited in a nearby parking lot for dawn. Dawn, so they could see what they were hitting with their lead-filled two-handed clubs.

The police in their hundreds came out of the parking lot on the run. They looked like movie actors in their riot gear. While photographers from the criminal justice branch took pictures from the rooftops, their locker mates waded into the crowd with mace and clubs and no thought of stopping until they reached the opposite corner.

My group was really what it claimed to be: pacifists. We had been directed to block one door of the induction centre by sitting in the street and on the sidewalk in a non-violent formation. A woman with a bullhorn led us in singing

I Ain't Gonna Study War No More and *We Shall Overcome*. When the police came, she positioned herself just beyond reach of the mace and the clubs.

"Get up and walk! Walk! Walk!" she yelled.

She looked like she had known all along that this would be the outcome, and wanted it and needed it to wake up a sleeping America. She looked thrilled and brave, and I instantly hated her for the joy took from the carnage behind her. All of my life that woman, who had shared the church basement with us, has been my metaphor for the kind of willingness to put people at risk that it takes to "heighten the contradictions." Or to stop a war. I hated her and I was in love with her. Her face stayed in my dreams for years.

She managed to move enough protestors blocking the road to create an escape route for everybody but those souls sitting right in front of the entrance. I had found garbage cans behind the building, and took a lid as a shield. When the crowd began to move away from the lines of police, I abandoned the sitting picket and entered the stream of people escaping the clubs.

A block away, we gathered behind automobiles that had been rolled over to create a barricade, like kids at a snowball fight. We left dozens of injured people behind for the paddy wagons, the hospitals and the jails.

That is when the riot truly began, and my time of doubt and wonder ended.

The slaughter that came with dawn became a running battle throughout downtown Oakland. As it extended from its epicentre, it drew in more people on their way to and from work.

Andy was standing on a street corner where demonstrators were told to disperse. When they didn't move fast enough, they were attacked and beaten. Sickened by the sight, he knelt to vomit, was dragged by his hair to a paddy wagon and taken to jail.

Block after block the policemen would form a line, tell people to pack up and go, then crunch down the street leaving human flotsam in their wake. "Mother" was a big help at this, grinding mechanically down the centrelines.

I was in the crowd, standing in front of a grocery store, when a dismounted squad of state patrolmen charged us. The building was held up by massive concrete pillars, and I stepped behind one of them in the hope that the cops would sweep past me. An old black woman carrying two bags of food came out of the store. She was dressed in hospital whites, obviously having finished a night shift somewhere, and had bought some groceries on her way home. Arms full, she was oblivious to what was happening. I yelled at her, and went to drag her back indoors just as the cops got there.

Two men in full battle dress hit her with their billyclubs, driving her sideways into the store's plate glass window. The window didn't break, and she bounced down the sidewalk without ever having seen what hit her. Forty cops were now running down the street, and this was the only citizen they could catch. She stumbled and her groceries spilled from the bags, and she and the men who beat her were tripping over oranges scattered on the pavement. If she hit the ground, they would have to leave her behind and have no outlet for their hatred, so they caught her by the arms. They lifted her back onto her feet, then hit her again – this time into a large litter bin that was on the corner. Again the cops caught her and stood her up.

I could no longer think of any use for the garbage lid "shield" I had been mindlessly carrying, so I dropped it, drawn along by the sheer sucking power of the violence in front of me.

Suddenly a young black man came at a full run from behind me. He scooped up the lid I had dropped and – time stretched out slowly here – spun it like a discus at one of the uniformed thugs beating the old woman who bought oranges. I heard the lid explode against the bottom of the cop's helmet where it met his neck, knocking him down. The young man darted away as all forty highway patrolmen looked around to see who had committed this assault on a fellow officer.

They saw me.

Not burdened with cans of mace, a flak jacket, combat boots, a helmet or club, I outran them.

They chased me for five blocks, but I ran for twenty.

I will never forget those twenty blocks. Into safety. Into the white community. Away from violence and into suburbia. Away from this awful crucible.

Across the country in Washington, D.C., my brother Lynden wound up on the roof of the Pentagon surrounded by the 7th Cavalry, or some such story. Later he went to New York for political activities, got beat up in Minneapolis for his weird appearance, and came back in bad shape to Oakland. Nobody knew if he was crazy or a genius in the wrong age.

In a moment of lucidity he found a job with the Greyhound company, acting as tour guide for a busload of Australian seniors going from Seattle to Chicago via Canada.

A few days after Lynden left on his trip with the Aussies, I got a phone call from the segregated YMCA where I taught black kids about filmmaking. My real dad, Phil, was there looking for me; he was a Public Defender – a lawyer with a conscience.

"We have to go to Canada and get your brother," he said.

Right from the beginning, Lynden had been too strange for the old folks. By the time they got to Vancouver, only a couple of hours north of Seattle, the bus driver wanted to get rid of him. When they drove east to Vernon, the driver asked a Mountie to talk to my brother, who by then had shut down completely. The poor constable walked up to Lynden in the bus station and put a hand on his shoulder in that kindly Canadian way that means *I am the authority here. Can I help you, or are you not what you appear to be?* And my brother, having had different experience with policemen, slugged him.

I learned this story from my dad on the highway north in his old green Cadillac that had the trunk fastened on with baling wire: Public Defenders aren't rich.

I also learned that the authorities in Vernon were treating Lynden as a violent and dangerous paranoid schizophrenic. He was in a hospital, but the nurses were refusing to look after him because they were scared. The hospital administration had hired full-time male attendants and, unless my dad could pay for them, we had better come to take their place. There was no talk of my brother being released to us.

I am not going to ever put on paper what happened in that hospital. It was horrible and it went on for days and I had to help them do it to him.

Lynden asked me for help, and I was too lost and too far from home and I didn't help him escape, and they took his memory away every day with electric shocks to his brain. And every day Phil would sit by his bed and rebuild Lynden's sense of who he was and where he came from until they had a whole person to torture again the next morning.

Cops came and searched our hotel room and our car, never telling us what they were looking for or why we were under suspicion. Phil and I split the days and nights, working 24 hours to keep the authorities from spending money for guards that he couldn't afford.

Someone finally said that Lynden was "subdued" enough to leave the hospital if we would drive him, drugged, straight to the border. In those days there was no easy way to head due south. I remember hours and hours of driving through the night before re-entering America at some tiny Washington state border crossing.

We were all starving; my brother was especially ravenous and grumpy as his drugs wore off. We spotted a glorified hamburger stand up ahead. It was called Shorty's, or something like that: one of those roadside diners that had a picnic table and a zoo, and velvet paintings and other junk to sell to the traveling public. We pulled in for something to eat. Nobody else was at the stand. There was a window where you ordered your food, and the menu was on the window. Phil went to the window first; got upset about something and walked away. Lynden and I went to the window and read the sign below the menu. It said, "Commies and hippie lovers not welcome."

The sign was offensive, but we were hungry. We ordered burgers and milkshakes. We had barely sat down to eat at the picnic table when our dad came back.

"Get in the car!" he said. There was anger in his voice.

He hadn't ordered us to do anything since we were children. I didn't move, so he grabbed my shirt, yanked me to my feet and threw me towards the car.

"Never mind the damned food!" he spit the words out.

We all piled into his Cadillac and burned out of the parking lot with tires squealing and gravel flying like kids on a Saturday night.

We drove in silence for a long time, nobody knowing what to say or how to begin until Phil started to giggle, then laugh. The tension broke and I asked him what the hell was going on.

"Some revolutionaries you guys are," he said. "You've got principles until your bellies are empty. Then you let anybody say hateful things to you as long as you can satisfy your immediate desires. You make me ashamed." But he was still laughing, so it was hard to get defensive.

"Where did you go when you read that sign?" I asked.

"I walked around back to get control of my temper," he said. "I found this bullshit little zoo full of snakes and raccoons and foxes and turtles. They didn't look any happier than me. I decided to open all the cages and let them out; cheer all of us up. I thought we'd better vacate the place before the owners saw their zoo walking down the highway."

In the end, my father left the United States before I did. He couldn't stand it anymore. He told all of his children to leave if they were able.

I wish we had some words like the Irish have "The Troubles" or the Palestinians have "The Intafada" for this madness you and I lived through. Never mind. Whatever we call it or don't call it, it is stuff that happened to people when our country tried to know itself.

Purple Haze

For years they held to their tree and the stars.
One night Lesser Panda followed a lamp down to the river,
Leaving Greater Panda to contemplate the dark.

Missoula

A lot of living and dying was packed into the next couple of circuits around the sun. I remember every detail except some of the time sequences. They are blurred because of all the enlightening and not-so-enlightening drugs I smoked, gulped, chewed, snorted, drank and cranked.

I learned a few things about them. Let me share.

This planet is full of drugs: some good, some bad, some free, some cheap, some expensive, some rare, some common, some addictive, some you'll refuse to take twice, some natural and some made in pharmaceutical factories. They can prevent polio or make you go blind, put you to sleep or keep you awake for days, save your life or end it.

From time to time people we don't know pick certain drugs to be legal and others to be outlawed. This is necessary in order to provide worldwide career opportunities for policemen, criminals, jailors, lawyers, judges and lawmakers who would otherwise have to become firemen, teachers, farmers or better cooks.

If you sell legal drugs, you are called a pharmacist. That's okay.

If you sell illegal drugs, you are called a pusher. That's not okay.

If you use legal drugs, you are called a consumer or a patient. That's okay.

If you use illegal drugs, you are called a doper or an addict. Not okay.

If you plant hops, you are called a farmer. Okay.

If you plant hemp, you are called a grower. Not okay.

Distill spirits in Saudi Arabia and you can be executed.

Distill spirits in America and your son can become President.

It's all wonderfully arbitrary, depending on what century and what country you are living in. There is no rhyme or reason for this, so you had best be your own judge of what works best for *you*. It will involve some trial and error. Good luck.

When marijuana came into town, I smoked my share. It made music a complete emotional experience. It revivified the languishing potato chip industry and added "munchies" to the lexicon. It provided a pleasant alternative definition of "stoned" to a word that used to only mean getting killed with rocks by an anonymous mob of bloodthirsty cretins.

Some folks know a gravy train when they see it. The marijuana-based employment sector now numbers more than a million in its symbiotic brotherhood of cops and crooks. Is it as strange to you as it is to me that neither the "good guys" nor the "bad guys" want us to legalize this thornless plant? It's all about money. The public admission of having enjoyed marijuana doesn't keep anybody from serving as a soldier or even a preacher (as long as he admits to being a miserable sinner). Candidates for public office and everyone crossing international borders, however, have to lie about having never inhaled its fumes. Talented and reliable employees have to perjure themselves with a drug disclaimer to get or keep a job. Most of us wink at the lie, but it is clever psychology: once we have been forced to lie, we will come to the defence of the lie instead of speaking the truth, which would expose the fact that we were cowardly lying sods in the first place. Few of us are courageous or cursed with a martyr complex. Meanwhile everyone makes bucks or spends bucks, has some fun, and hopes that only the slow-witted get caught. Politically, the fuss about "grass" was another illustration to me of how profoundly illogical, convoluted and amoral society really is.

For those few of you who never had any, hashish is to marijuana what espresso is to regular grind. Casual smokers bought it by the gram rather than the much larger one ounce baggie that was *de rigeur* for pot. When you got stopped by the cops for having long hair and driving around Circle Square, you could avoid waste and arrest by swallowing the hash; baggies of weed had to be slyly tossed out of the car window into the gutter or into the hands of any lucky teen happening to pass by on the sidewalk.

In 1966 you could order hashish by mail with relatively small risk of getting busted. The biggest chance you took was that of your "key" (a kilogram block made a worthwhile package) disappearing in transit. Those wily postal workers! A lot of them were young too. One of them had a finely balanced sense of ethics – a delivery that we had ordered from California arrived having been opened and resealed. Half the expected key was missing, but there was a note. It said: *The US Postal Service has randomly selected this item to undergo mandatory quality control testing. This may result in some loss of product. Your shipment is hereby certified as Superior quality.*

We wrote an unsigned thank-you note to the San Francisco postmaster.

LSD was one of the finest drugs ever developed by the US government. It gave you fresh and colourful perspectives on everything. Chairs smell. People talk through their eyes. You can see music; wander in wonder around a willing friend's body for an eternal day.

The East Front gang was initially careful about its acid trips; everybody had a "guide" to make sure the "tripper" didn't drink furniture polish like my brother once did as a curious three year-old. Before long, though, we dispensed with the guide and ate it like popcorn, or drank it dissolved in Kool-Aid or Tang or cheap wine. After the 110th consecutive day of dropping acid, I stopped keeping track of my trips.

God never revealed Itself to me in Its entirety while I was stoned on LSD, but I did have the tag football game of my life when the Hash Freaks challenged us Acid Heads to play for a couple of cases of beer. It was all on the up and up, with more effective drug-testing than you get in the Olympics or the *Tour de France* or major league baseball; only with us you *had* to be on drugs.

The Freaks arrived early on the field with trays of hash brownies. A mutually trusted third party volunteered to eat some and soon assured both teams that the brownies were good in every way. She then volunteered to drink a glass of Electric Kool-Aid that we'd made for our team. An hour later she couldn't assure anybody of anything. Having proofed the drugs (I refer you to *I Thessalonians 5:21*), the Freaks gobbled theirs and we chugged ours and we all started playing football.

The Freaks took a 14-7 halftime lead, licked their dessert trays clean and sent their baker off down the 93 Strip with orders for burgers and fries. Our quarterback called us together.

"We're playing like a bunch of dopers out there," he began. It was hard to disagree. "Look at me," he said. We did. His pupils were dilated to the size of hubcaps. We all fell down laughing. He concluded his speech while lying on his back. "We can do better. The other team is stoned on hash for Chrissakes! This isn't just any game – this is for beer!" Beer was highly prized. Unlike the drugs we were on, it cost money, and you had to pretend to be twenty-one to buy it.

With the QB's inspiring words clanging like Moravian iron church bells in our skulls, we returned to the field. If you put your mind to snatching cloth flags out of other people's pants, you could do it real well on LSD. Our defense tightened. I caught a pass running the world's slowest post pattern, and scored a touchdown because the Freak's safety got distracted by the late arrival of his hamburgers. Tracking that ball as it sailed frame by strobe-lit frame over my head and into my hands was one of those cheesy Hall of Fame moments I like to recall when I splatter spaghetti sauce over a clean shirt for the umpteenth time.

A drawback of hashish is that you can fall victim to the sweet thought that your good intentions are simply not worth the effort needed to achieve them; that it's time for a snack break. Peaking on our trips in the second half of the game, the Acid Heads blocked and ran and jinked around as if possessed, while the Freaks started moseying over to the sidelines to watch the game instead of playing it. We could hear them chewing French fries and burping.

We won 49-14; shared the beer in the Freaks' end zone. Missoula was a college town after all, and back then you could get away with drinking in public as long as you didn't smash the bottles or give any to the grade school kids who always hung around hoping that you would.

Blotter acid was fine, but the slickest was called Windowpane. The LSD was put onto little squares of transparent cellulose or cornstarch; at least it melted on your tongue. The first batch we ever got was said to be Owsley acid that came from the Grateful Dead. The Dead was the country's greatest psychedelic band. Owsley was the nation's greatest psychedelic chemist. They all lived around San Francisco. The Dead was booked to do a show in Missoula, but had to cancel. A small cardboard box holding a thousand hits of Windowpane showed up by way of an apology. That's professionalism. That's concern for your fans.

On the opposite side of the fence was Andy Warhol. The famous pop artist came to town for a few days. The university's art crowd outdid itself to wine and dine him and his entourage. A surprising number had met him before, and got to reminisce. For ten grand he even addressed a hastily organized convocation of 1500 admirers at the campus theater. I went, but left after five minutes because he was just standing at the lectern like he was waiting for somebody to speak to *him*. It was a good joke. He made an even better one a month later when the Associated Press ran a story of how Warhol had hired an impersonator and some New York street people to tour several podunk western colleges in his place.

Love them or hate them, trust them or not, Warhol and the Grateful Dead could take you for a ride.

There was cocaine in town, and it was a tolerably decent, very expensive drug with a ridiculously short flight time. I only knew it was expensive because people would say how much they had paid for it while they cut me free lines on a pocket mirror. Among ourselves drug dealing was a non-profit business: enough was sold to rich clients that East Front could have fully subsidized pharmaceuticals. We called it Missoula Pharmacare.

You could shoot coke right into your veins after "flagging", but it was considered more sophisticated to snort lines of it up your nose through a twenty dollar bill and look for somebody to ball. Too much for too long would wreck your mucous membranes and the rest of your life. "Tooting" was pretty addictive, partly because you crashed so badly after an hour. The one thing that saved my ass, when it came to cocaine, was strict adherence to the Scottish principle of never buying the stuff.

Strange to say, the only hallucinogens I ever paid for were the legal ones: Romilar cough syrup, Heavenly Blue morning glory seeds and ground nutmeg. The first was sold over-the-counter at every drug store, the second at most garden shops, the third at any reputable grocery. They were Rummel's drugs of choice, and a more God-awful assortment of brain-numbing garbage would be hard to find.

I began dropping over to Jay's place after the peace march. Naked women were always there. He was carving a mammoth woodcut called *Ghost Dance*. Its left side depicted the rise of the mighty plains Indian, the right side his descent to cigar store and wino status. The centre showed his apotheosis as a medicine man dancing beneath a flying stallion ridden by a female nude. Every girl on East Front and half of Kappa Omicron Pi must have posed for Rummel while he carved that figure. They would undress and sit on a saddle thrown over a sawhorse, turned towards him and smoking joints while his carving knives moved ever so carefully and slowly.

"What does the female figure represent?" I asked.

"Women," he said, licking his chops.

On warm nights in the summer of '66 we would carry our guitars downtown and play music outside the bars or around Circle Square, which was a traffic circle at the north end of Higgins where it was blocked by the freightyards. Jay had a battered Sears & Roebuck Stella 12-string with wornout frets and brutal action. He didn't play it as much as beat on it. It was real loud, like the way he sang. We never put out a hat or a guitar case into which passersby could chuck coins. We wailed away out of pure joy.

Performing with him took some getting used to: at his insistence we'd each drink a bottle of Romilar (he called it "Karl"), then eat a package of morning glory seeds or gag down a mug of dried ground nutmeg before heading out. The codeine cough syrup was a skid row stone. The Heavenly Blues were trippy if we washed off the chemicals the seed companies had to put on them to make us puke and stop eating them. Jay loved nutmeg; would grin and say it made him feel the blues. It made me feel like I'd smoked DMT and fallen through a Woody Street sewer grate. We soon agreed that magic mushrooms were an acceptable substitute.

Ah, magic mushrooms! Except for Athlete's Foot, those perfect little taupe cones are the only fungi I have ever been able to identify with confidence. I liked them more than peyote buttons, which would knock me to my knees and make me think that everybody was speaking Spanish or Yaqui. I don't understand Spanish or Yaqui, but the colours of those languages are deep and bright.

Opium balls feel tacky to the touch and smoke well in small pipes. A bonus with opium was that if you got too blitzed you could close your eyes and nod off anywhere without discomfort. It's the drug for couch surfers. With the help of opium and codeine Rudy Johnson lived on top of the refrigerator in Oz's alley shack for three days and nights, refusing to come down until Oz scraped together enough money to fix Rudy's stereo.

Oswald 'Oz' Peterson was a gangly young graduate of Missoula's Hellgate High. Remember that name. We soon got to be close friends; he even became a father of my oldest daughter, and...I'll explain later. Rudy had forced him into accepting the loan of the stereo in the first place. It was for a party that involved repeatedly bumping it off the free-standing antique oak fireplace mantle that Oz had bought on a whim, and which occupied most of what passed as the living room. Poor Rudy had a predilection for violence and sadism, sometimes ameliorated by a massive intake of opiates and barbituates. I was saddened by his early suicide, but have always admired his decision to remove himself from the picture before he did more irreparable damage to many innocents. Rudy was sick and crazy, yet in the end he had the jam to do what was right.

"Downers" like Qualude, Valium and phenobarbital were most popular among the unhappy people in grad school and the wives of the local loggers. Because they were made by the world's *real* drug cartel – the international pharmaceutical industry – they were legal and easy to get with a prescription. I didn't care for them; they made me drowsy; always thought there must be some in MDA, an otherwise fine psychedelic that never grabbed the public's imagination. Poor marketing? Lack of an influential German backer? Factory explosions? How could Thalidomide make the cut while MDA failed? It's a strange world.

I never used heroin, although I suppose I should have at least tried some – like the way cops today shoot each other with Tasers to "get a feel" for it.

"Uppers" were my drugs. Here's my quick version of their development. Even trained soldiers prefer not to fight those who possess the power to retaliate in kind. For millennia the rank and file went into battle drunk, and were tolerably effective at eviscerating each other at close range with swords and pikes. By the time of the world wars of the 20th century, artillerymen, aerial bombardiers and even infantrymen could kill well at a distance if they were sober enough to focus on their mechanical aids. The trouble with sober mortal combat is that it's not popular among the participants; military psychology studies reported that even a few hours of shooting men and women – and getting shot at yourself – made you very tired and sleepy, like being on the back side of a big drunk. This was bad. So benzedrine was manufactured and issued to troops to keep them awake and intent on the job at hand without even getting hungry. It was cheap to make and worked like a dream. After the wars the drug companies looked around for a civilian market for this profitable moneymaker. They found it in the American housewife, the American trucker, the American doctor and the American college student. Slightly reconfigured into a variety of patented methamphetamines, a generation of pills and capsules had mom whistling through hours of vacuuming, dusting, cooking and raising the kids – looking trim and with energy left to keep dad up half the night. Truckers could stay at the wheel babbling non-stop over their citizens' band radios. Doctors were submerged in free samples, and loved them. Hundreds of lives were saved, and a few lost, by speed-crazed physicians and surgeons. Collegians liked them because they allowed you to goof off for most of an academic term, then stay up for hours cramming for your finals.

Marybeth turned me onto speed. She was a good mentor. "Try one of these," she said. "Remember to eat, even if you're not hungry. Drink lots of water and juice. Lie down, close your eyes and rest every night, even if you don't sleep. Have fun! Let me know if you want some more. I've got three prescriptions for them."

The next day I let her know that I had found my drug. I kept a bowlful of pills by my mattress. I found a natural holistic balance between the need for sleep and the desire to be awake and "happening" by regularly lying down to rest at 2 a.m., setting an alarm clock for 5 a.m., when I'd do a dex and go back to sleep until the pill woke me up humming at full throttle at 6 o'clock.

Methedrine was more subtle and dangerous. You could swallow or snort or shoot crystal and feel on top of the world without wanting to do a blessed thing. It ruined a lot of promising people. "Cranking" seemed to be the most destructive. I remember taking away a friend's syringe as he sat on a toilet hitting up for the third time in an hour trying to "get off." He was so freaking speeded that he'd lost all track of his injections, or any sense of sanity.

Although I felt bound to try it, I always thought that intravenous drug use was a little seedy and unhealthy; however, it did give Enoch experience that came in handy when the East Front gang went to donate blood. The young daughter of some friends was having heart surgery in Seattle. If we gave blood, they would get credited with that many units toward their daughter's transfusions. We all quit dope for 72 hours in order to pass on as pure a product as we could to future unsuspecting recipients, then headed to the Red Cross clinic. We must have made the attendant male nurse nervous; he was inept at finding our veins – some of which were truly virgin. It took him three attempts before he got into mine. Enoch watched in disgust. Then the nurse fumbled his first try with Marybeth. Enoch grabbed the syringe, pushed him aside and said, "Here, let me." His needle slid in effortlessly. Marybeth smiled. The nurse was so stunned that he didn't call the police or throw us out.

The attendant might not have been great with a "point," but he came through like a trooper when we started fainting. It seems that most of us hadn't had the time or money to eat well recently, and we felt the blood loss more than most donors. He was adjusting clamps and feeding us orange juice and donuts like a madman for a while. Duly fed and bled, we thanked him and stumbled home.

The surgery was successful and our friends moved to Canada, settling in a place called the Slocan Valley.

Speaking of eating well, nobody I knew did. One guy went 31 days on nothing but Great Falls Select and mozzarella cheese before collapsing. He was tenderly dumped off at the campus infirmary, soon recovered and went on to own a fried chicken franchise in White Sulphur Springs.

My favorite diner wasn't the Oxford or The Top Hat, but an All You Can Eat For 99 Cents truckstop out in Bonner. It served edible bulk food, and a few of us drove there to chow down every week until the management – out of necessity – told the waitresses to take away our plates and silverware after our second trips to the buffet. We still dropped in regularly because, if Norma was the waitress, for fifty cents you could order coffee with Dexedrine on the side. Most of the patrons seemed to be in favor of bombing the hell out of Hanoi, but we all shared a love for mashed potatoes, lime Jell-O and speed. It was a fine place.

That Ol' Missoula Moon

The moon rises atrociously over Missoula.

She is an hour later than predicted, and lucky at that. Trying to come up through Hellgate she is gassed over the Bonner mill, then slapped back into Rock Creek by the wind. At Jackpine Ranch Bitterroot Al and his gal Sal see her having trouble and suggest she come in farther south, over Mount Sentinel.

This she does, and things are going alright until she reaches the summit. Folks looking out of their car windows on the 93 Strip see her graze the crest too closely and high-centre on a rock fracture called the Eagle's Nest.

Embarrassed, straining, and feeling close to bust, the damaged goddess moon finally jerks free and trips right into a coulee.

That's where Rummel, hanging out with one of Sentinel's two mythical blue pandas, is waiting for her. He spends half his nights chasing her. Wouldn't you know it – the one evening she stumbles into his lap he is wrecked on nutmeg and Karl. Even so, he almost jumps the old girl. Misses by inches, but nobody has ever come so close.

Distressed beyond measure, now praying only to get unseen through this sacrilegious valley, the moon skitters towards the Clark Fork. With a train of light turned hem-out and hiked around her waist she enters the flowing water.

From the sticky poplar shadows at the mouth of Rattlesnake Creek the East Front gang passes the wine and the hash pipe as they watch her steal red-faced through town. A few minutes later Rummel and a happy Chinese sloth swim by singing loudly in her wake.

Marybeth's Song

The wallpaper breathes soft budding roses, and mist from the petals will swirl through her room. The mirror is full of water. The doorway is hung with linen. A breeze twirls through her window, shimmering fragrant air.

Marybeth lies quiet now on her bed with Myra, who must be sleeping: two smooth-flanked milk-nude lovers, languorous inside a flower. A spring of swallows sails through green gauze curtains while Marybeth traces a world of fingertips on the body of her friend.

Light harmonies ripple down the bed sheets and across their slick-running thighs. Long hair, forever unribboned, lays wild across the bed. Myra smiles in her dream when Marybeth's fingers glide slowly up the inside of her legs in mirrors or rosebuds, or woven cloth, and all the swallows in the air.

Reality Is

Eventually I recalled that there is more to life than being drunk and stoned.

For example, there is the need to pay the rent and feed yourself. That required money, even on East Front. Until the summer of '66 I remained employed as a dishwasher by the U of M food service. I'd taken it on as another part-time job at the start of the school term. When the administration fired me as an RA, it forgot to fire me as a dishwasher. I ran a machine that steamed and sterilized 3000 plates an hour, but my favorite task was scraping the dishes as they came in from the cafeteria on a rubber delivery belt; I could highgrade the best leftovers and put them into a plastic bag to bring home for everybody. Relatively untouched baked potatoes and meat carried well, and were popular. The same could not be said of mashed potatoes or chocolate pudding.

That job was tied to the school year. When it ended, I hired on with Go Ed Janitors. Ed was a man who had bought a second hand Dodge van that had the customary DODGE metal letters on its grill. He rearranged them to read GO ED, hence the company name. He kept the extra D as a spare in case the first one ever fell off. I was his only employee. He was a great boss who had been drinking too much for years. His dream was to get a pilot's license. I don't know if he ever succeeded, but I know he took lessons because he once invited me to fly with him and his instructor. That was my first time in a plane. The instructor had him bump our Cessna into the brown pall of sulfurous smog above the Frenchtown mill, then practice circling at a steady height. Having failed to do that, the instructor took him back over the airport to practice "touch and go" landings and takeoffs. Ed had a lot of "go," but not much "touch." On his last run, the instructor had to take over the controls to keep us from piling into some Herefords that were grazing four hundred yards short of the runway. There was a controller in the airport tower, doing his job in Montana fashion: *Whiskey Hotel Yankee Four Two Niner, you're coming in too low. Repeat, too low. Livestock at twelve o'clock, cowboys.*

Having temporarily dealt with the need to keep myself fed and watered, it was possible to spend much of each day working with others to correct America's moral compass. I helped to organize a demonstration against local realtors who didn't make their rental properties available to the few black students the college Athletic Director imported to add finesse and urban flair to our ball teams. Although their ancestors may have once been enslaved, then segregated and treated like trash, Afro-Americans were never so desperate as to come to Montana to herd sheep or mine the hills of Anaconda and Butte. They *would* come to play basketball in a heated pavilion.

Our committee spent a week coming up with a name to call ourselves for this project to promote social justice; then with a newspaperman, three radio reporters and a television crew in tow, we randomly selected a realty company to picket in order to shine a public spotlight on systemic racism in the Big Sky.

This was not wise.

The company we had so casually picked had the most liberal and fair-minded policies and rental records you will ever find. If you are looking to target someone in order to raise a public issue, I suggest that you don't do it on the basis of random selection. We looked suitably stupid, and had slagged some nice people.

We might have slunk away in shame, but we were Americans. We quickly disbanded to make it harder for our victim to sue us, then started up again under a new name.

College dropouts like me rightfully lost their military draft deferments and became reluctant grist for the mill of American geopolitics. Until you were officially summoned for service, you were classified as 1A and had to carry an identity card with you at all times or risk imprisonment. Burning your draft card was more than a symbolic gesture – in Montana it carried a stiffer legal penalty than fucking sheep or being convicted of vehicular homicide.

I applied for 1A0 status: that of Conscientious Objector. You could still be drafted, but you didn't have to kill people. It was a way to accommodate Quakers,

Amish and other purists who actually followed the tenets of their sissy religions. And, honestly, it's a good concept. To my surprise, I got it – even though the guy who did my applicant interview described me as "completely irreligious." I either had a fan on the Thurston County draft board, or it was done as a favor in honour of Dad's distinguished service record.

Being 1A0 didn't stop my growing involvement in the anti-war movement. The more I read about my country's self-serving chicanery in Southeast Asia, the madder I got. We were on the wrong side in this conflict. And most Americans knew it. Our people's disgrace was to put aside our democratic and revolutionary antecedents in the interests of a career with Dow Chemical and a dream lifetime in suburbia. It looked more and more like Woodrow Wilson's ecstatically naïve Fourteen Points, and our later founding of the United Nations would mark the apogee of the American empire; we were now on the far side of greatness.

Missoula County boys were bused over the Rockies to Butte for their induction physical. If they passed, they returned home to await orders to boot camp. The ones who failed went back to Eddy's Club to get drunk and celebrate. I decided to get on those buses and offer their riders some unmilitary options.

It was easy to make contact with people in Canada and Sweden who would help dodgers get into their country, legally or otherwise. It was easy to get you to California and put you in touch with reputable crooks who could provide the basics of a new identity if that's what you wanted. It was easy to line up legal counsel if you wanted to straight-up challenge the morality or legality of the war and then go to jail as a sincere American. It was easy to set up a free cab service to take you straight to the hospital if you wanted to first shoot yourself in the foot or chop off your trigger finger. Enoch even volunteered to shoot you if you didn't want to do it yourself.

It was harder to get on the bus. You had to have induction papers before the rotating recruiting sergeants would let you board. They were then in charge of feeding and billeting and ordering you around until your return.

Kids who didn't want to go to Vietnam soon learned that our group might help them. Some of them chose to bail and go to California; we helped many more get into Canada. In either case, I'd ask them to give me their induction notices, which I'd take to the Greyhound depot and present to what always seemed to be a new recruiting sergeant. I would ride to Butte, passing out information sheets and talking to the riders about ways to flunk the army physical or temporarily disappear or immigrate to a better country. I expected to have the hell beat out of me by the recruiter or my fellow passengers. That never happened. Maybe it was because we were all reluctant soldiers. I do know that within a few years over 30% of inductees simply weren't showing up for their physicals, and that says something about the war's popular support. Even the sergeants were non-violent, although a couple took me aside and said they could hardly wait for me to be sworn into the army.

And *that* never happened because when we got to Butte I'd eat the free dinner, take a shower in the hotel room that was provided, then hitchhike back to Missoula. I only stayed overnight once, talking with a kid from Hamilton who was torn about what to do with his life. We both left the lineup in the morning, suffering the sergeant's taunts but knowing that he couldn't stop us as long as we were civilians. The kid later had another change of heart and turned himself into the recruiting depot. I guess you could say he was conflicted.

The FBI thought the anti-war movement was un-American. It sent another undercover agent to infiltrate our motley crew. He drove into town in a blue 1962 Ford Fairlane with Custer County plates. We knew that because Myra and some other friends were switchboard operators at the phone company and always listened in on their calls.

We were there to introduce ourselves, say hello and take his picture when he arrived at the Federal building. Bitterroot Al paid to have the picture enlarged and put onto posters which we plastered around the city. Underneath the mug shot the poster read: ***Do you know this man? He may be posing as an FBI agent. If you see him near children or school grounds, please report him to the Missoula Police Department.***

The MPD got dozens of calls about the guy. Parents organized to tail him everywhere he went. He lasted about a week before being recalled.

Bitterroot Al, by the way, was the financier of first resort whenever we really needed money for the peace movement. Someone said he was a ninth cousin to Jeanette Rankin, the state's famous feminist and pacifist. Through quirks of fate she was the only member of the US Congress to vote against America's participation in both world wars. Now in her eighties, she was still alive and making plans to lead the 5000-member Jeanette Rankin Brigade in a march on Washington, which she did in '68. Al kept a lower profile as befitted a spurious relative and the kingpin of the Missoula Mafia.

He and his gal Sal owned Jackpine Ranch, a sweet little 160-acre spread up Rock Creek. No, he didn't cultivate marijuana there. The ranch was for Jersey milk cows and some Berkshire Spotted pigs that Sal thought were cuddly. He didn't cultivate marijuana at all. He was the owner of a 92' schooner that could regularly be seen full of bananas off the Leeward Islands or Bimini or – sometimes at sunset – off Key West. He loved that boat, as well as BMW cars and motorcycles, which he imported from Germany with their gas tanks full of hashish. He didn't deal in hard drugs. Sal was a reformed junkie. Al didn't have employees; he had friends. In turn, they and their families had full and free Blue Cross medical coverage, a modest dental plan and access to a substantial legal defense fund if they were busted. He was a great judge of character. Nobody ever ratted on Al because he had nothing to do with anyone who might. I am only telling you this now that he and Sal are beyond the reach of the law; they died in an avalanche while skiing together near Aspen a few years ago.

I still smile to think that the FBI said there were links between organized crime and the anti-war movement. Like that takes brains to figure out. Next thing you know the Bureau will suspect that there are links between organized crime and state and national governments. I'm proud to have known Bitterroot Al, who could always be counted on to come up with enough money to get a kid out of the state and either underground or into Canada. We never asked for more.

Marybeth's Whiskey

Marybeth breathes Woody Street. She knows Fat Maria, drinks bourbon and likes the country music at the Sunshine Bar. She knows the railroad tracks and back alleys behind Circle Square.

She can sing with a row of derelicts.

There is a legless man who begs outside the false-front Revival Mission. Marybeth gives him anything but money. One time she cries.

He wears her scarf.

Twice she tells him to screw himself.

Once, behind a toolshed in the Northern Pacific freight yard, she gives him a fuck for his last dime because he coughs blood and tells her he still has standards.

Come a Wreck

December arrived with its usual load of sleet and snow. At my parents' invitation I drove to the coast on a pocketful of speed in a borrowed Volkswagen to spend Christmas with the family. I wasn't especially gracious about coming home, arriving after dark on Christmas Eve and leaving on Boxing Day.

Mom hugged me when I got there; so did Fay and Ken. My sister was at the top of her high school class; my brother was playing guitar with his teeth as well as his thumbs. He was already a better guitarist than I would ever be. Maybe someday he would try using his fingers. Dad and I pulled our punches, bit our lips and still managed to butt heads about my future. He saw it to be bleak; I saw it as ethically correct, unknown and exciting. We were both right; a father and son with irreconcilable points of view.

It was raining when I left; snowing across the Cascades; windy, gray and miserable through eastern Washington. Passing semis blew the Volkswagen around like a cheap tin can. I had run out of pep pills and got drowsy, but ate the sandwich Mom had made for me and kept going.

The Idaho panhandle was choked with sleet and ice. I was very sleepy; started to nod off; stuck my head out the window to wake up. The trip had been a bummer. I dreamed of getting back to 809 East Front and the bat that had flown into my apartment to die and dessicate on the window curtain...

...I woke up to find myself still on the road, steadfastly purring straight as an arrow towards the front grill of an oncoming car. I was in the wrong lane.

Head-on is death. Jerk the wheel. Oops! Too much. That was badly done. Well, shit...

...The motorist I didn't kill stopped when the Volkswagen cartwheeled into a telephone pole. Good thing I'd flown out the door along the way. He covered me up with a duffel coat and flagged down a trucker to call on his CB radio for an ambulance. Thanks, folks. That was real dumbass driving on my part.

The staff at the Smelterville hospital waited for my internal hemorrhages to show themselves. There weren't any; just a broken back, and I could move all my body parts. The only lasting damage was to the nerves in my legs. I still twitch and ripple 24 hours a day. And for years if I turned or bent exactly right, the traumatized muscles would knot up and make me fall down.

My mother showed up the next day – the ambulance attendant had made certain to get the information about my next-of-kin and medical coverage. I wasn't supposed to move yet, so had to lie in bed while she hired a barber to come in and cut my hair. It was a control thing, and only the tip of the iceberg. She stayed the time it took for me to get fitted with a leather-padded steel back brace that I was told to wear for six months. Then Dad drove out to pick us both up and drag my sorry self back to Lacey. He must have paid the hospital bills because I never got any.

Life was strange there. Dad took my wallet away. It held my driver's license, some money and ID cards. Mom called a minister to make house calls to save my soul and talk about the evils of drugs. Fay and Ken were always sent out of the room when I'd start to argue that it was America's soul, not mine, that needed saving; that two-faced people were a greater evil than mind-altering plants.

Dad told Mom to lock me in the house if I had to be left alone; bought some padlocks for the purpose. Their intent was clear: I was going to be reprogrammed. Psychological reprogramming takes place when people who don't like what you're thinking suck out *your* brain and replace it with *theirs.* This makes for social cohesion, but we know that zombies and lynch mobs are socially cohesive; the fact that they can easily interact with one another doesn't make their victims feel any better.

It was scary. Had this been my home? Were these my parents or interplanetary aliens? Was this my country? Was life only a veneer hiding such emptiness of spirit?

Dad went to work each morning; Fay and Ken went to school. Mom wouldn't leave me alone for days, but finally padlocked me into the house while she did some grocery shopping or spent another mortgage payment on clothes.

I searched the place until I found my wallet, contents intact, then climbed backwards very gingerly onto the kitchen counter and out the window. The brace made it awkward and I didn't want to snap my spine a second time. Jailbreak.

I headed for Missoula like a homing pigeon.

Oren's Daughter

Oren Jones and his wife Wanda had three daughters. Mae was the oldest. The youngest, Delia, wore a variety of wacky dresses, all pink, was still in high school and worked at a hamburger stand. They were all attractive in every sense of the word, but my eyes were on Beryl.

She had long black hair, opposed the war in Vietnam, dressed like a beatnik, was smart as a whip, had a prescription for birth control pills, ignored spinal supports and liked to ball. Aside from a love of edgy poetry, the beatnik thing was a pose: she was always trying to improve herself. Second-child syndrome? This was a shame because she was by nature one of the finest people I've met.

She was a freshman at U of M. She and Delia lived at home in a cloud of boyfriends who hung in the air like blackflies around raw meat. The Oz and I were two of them. Oz said that Oren was a long-haul trucker with a quick temper, especially if he caught you messing with his girls. Messing? Within a month of getting back to town I was spending more nights in her upstairs bedroom than at my own place. I would sneak in after her mom went to sleep and tiptoe out before dawn. There were no dead bats on Beryl's curtains.

Oren and his big White diesel had been freighting in the Midwest, so Wanda had dreamt alone and I had slept with his daughter for a good while before he got a load that brought him back through the valley.

Wanda was a tolerant parent, and I was part of the usual pack of idlers hanging out at the house one evening when the front door opened and a barrel-chested man walked in as if he owned the place. He didn't – the bank did – but he was the better part of drunk, and he looked proprietorial enough. Oren was back.

Wanda and the girls ran to give him hugs and kisses. He sized up the rest of us useless dogs.

"Howdy. Y'all got one minute to get outta here."

The useless dogs bid quick adieus. Most scuttled through the back door. One hid in the basement. I stuck around. I wasn't going to leave unless Beryl asked me. It's part of the mating ritual.

He walked right up to my face.

"Who the heck are you?" he asked.

"I'm Gary, one of Beryl's friends." I waited for his knuckles or the boots.

He glanced at his middle daughter for confirmation. She nodded. He seemed to be considering a load of new information.

"Are you one of them guitar player guys?"

"Yup."

"Can you play *Blue Moon of Kentucky*?"

"In any key you want."

"How 'bout D? I got an ol' D harp somewhere. You like beer?"

Oren was a mighty piece of cosmic engineering. After almost a half century and a lot of water under the bridge, we're still good friends. I swamped for him on a few trips, riding along to clean out cattle trailers, load and unload vegetables, and keep the fake logbook for the Interstate Commerce Commission – the one all the truckers kept, which showed that they slept regularly and never worked overtime. Except for that logbook he was honest to a fault, full of entrepreneurial spirit, forever going broke and starting over again from scratch like he'd done as a young man come north from Texas.

I rode to Portland, Oregon, with him in a battered old truck – he'd had to sell the White. The clutch began packing it in at the start of the trip, so Oren drove all the way without using it, showing me how you can shift through the gears smooth as butter if you know your engine and the road and your gear ratios.

He was a man's man, but he liked women a whole lot too. I suppose that was one of the reasons he and Wanda broke up for a while after the girls left home. Beryl and I went with him to a bar in Ravalli. She and I were under the legal drinking age but nobody asked us for ID when we were with Oren. We had a few beers and he decided to show me how a gentleman asks a lady for a dance at a bar. Flustered, I looked to Beryl for help, but she only grinned. After all, she'd grown up with him.

He first reconnoitered the room. "See that ol' girl over there?" he whispered. "She's got a weddin' ring, but she's a'playin' with it. She'll dance if ya ask her. That one next to her won't. She's with one o' them guys shootin' pool – the one that keeps eyeballin' us." He scanned the barstools. "Now, by golly, there's a good-looker. The brunette. But don't ask the prettiest one first. Puts everybody on edge. Work your way up to it. Besides, the prettiest one ain't always the best dancer. Here's how you do it."

He pulled a comb from his jeans, slicked down his hair and sauntered to the jukebox, dropped in a quarter and picked three country and western favorites. Under the scrutiny of the patrons, he walked over to the "ol' girl," clapped his hands behind his back in cowboy fashion and said loudly enough for everyone to hear, "Howdy, ma'am. My name is Oren Jones. I come by way of Texas. A good-lookin' woman like you shouldn't be sittin' here while there's music playin'. Would you do me the honour of takin' a spin around the floor?" Then he leaned closer to her and said something nobody else could hear. She giggled like a schoolgirl and let him escort her to the dance floor where they both swung easily into the classic western steps.

The brunette took more convincing, but they shared a dance after I saw him point Beryl and me out to her. He came back to our table looking pretty satisfied with himself.

"What did you say to her, Oren?" I asked.

"Well, you could see the cute one wasn't much interested in ol' fellers like me. I had to tell her I was teachin' my daughter's boyfriend how to ask a beautiful woman for a dance." He shook his head. "Sometimes you gotta be flexible in your approach."

Then it was my turn. I put on some music; dutifully stood in front of Beryl and asked her for "the honour," but skipped the behind-the-back-handclasp part. She said yes anyhow. Neither of us knew how to two-step, so we did a playground shuffle to the politely muted professional disappointment of every dancer in the bar except for her father. The song I had selected to tease my partner was Tammy Wynette's *Stand by Your Man*. As Tammy called on all women to support their hard-working yahoos who did things that a woman can't understand, Beryl put her lips to my ear and said, "You owe me for this."

Although there wasn't a mean bone in Oren's body, Oz was right in saying that he had a quick temper. For a while he drove short-haul for a gyppo outfit logging up Pattee Canyon. Turnaround time from the landing to the mill was important if you didn't want to go bust; the route brought you racing through town and north across the river on the Higgins Street bridge. You could also cross the Clark Fork on Reserve Street or Russell or Madison, but Higgins was the most direct.

Wanda had invited Oz and me over for supper, so we were there when Oren came home looking troubled. Gathered around a table of hot spaghetti, she asked him how his day had been.

"I won't lie. It was darned rough," he said. He never swore. "I got in a fight with some of your friends, Beryl. I'm real sorry, but I lost my temper."

He told us that there had been another anti-war demonstration, a small one that culminated in a knot of protestors closing down the south ramp onto the bridge. He and his load of logs were stuck in the ensuing traffic snarl.

"Y'all know I got nothin' against peace and Vietnam, but those boys was holdin' up my rig, and that's not right."

"Oren, what did you do to those kids?" Wanda asked sternly.

"Well, honey, I asked 'em real polite to let me through."

"And...?"

"They wouldn't."

"So...?"

"I had to move 'em out of the way."

Out of the way? He had cold-cocked two of them before throwing a couple more off the ramp and down the riverbank. Guys only; he wouldn't hurt a girl. Having cleared the congestion on the bridge, he climbed back into his rig and finished his run while the police arrived to arrest the survivors for parading without a license.

It had been a dumb stunt, but no one was permanently injured. And, to their credit, no one ever thought of pressing charges against Beryl Jones's dad – they all accepted the fact that you made him mad at your own risk. That was Oren for you.

When you're young, entire eras come and go with rapidity. The East Front scene faded even as its acolytes spread across the city and beyond like a big burp.

Marybeth went into semi-seclusion to complete her Master's degree in Performing Arts. Enoch remained firmly rooted on East Front, but Rummel pulled up stakes and moved to San Francisco, where he found new inspiration and still more models in Haight-Ashbury. To help Jay get traveling money, I gave him $20 for a hand-tinted copy of his *Ghostdance* woodcut which he had finally completed and printed with ink that he kept in his bathtub. That left me with $18 until I could sell the last of my textbooks – Ed had to lay me off work when I cracked my back.

Oz invited me to stay with him in a converted 1930s alley garage that his mother owned off Arthur Street. Rent was free, and it was close to Beryl's house. Dame Fortune beamed her pointy face my way. The place was busy and cluttered with knick-knacks, the monster oak fireplace mantle, a glazed clay wine barrel that doubled as an ashtray, and Rudy occasionally living on top of the refrigerator.

Oz was a ramshackle, haphazard and uncoordinated 6'5" and had failed the road test for his driver's license a half dozen times, most recently breaking the tail light of another car and backing onto the sidewalk into a parking meter when he tried to parallel park. Beryl and I spent hours with him behind the wheel of Oren's pickup and Wanda's DeSoto to improve his skills for another assault on Motor Vehicles.

He passed on his seventh test, in a winter snowstorm, using the DeSoto. We were all happy. Not that she didn't trust him, but Beryl drove the car home. It took some time to get there because Oz had her stop to give a ride to a frozen bum who was thumbing a ride outside the Florence Hotel. The man pitched, reeking, into the back seat, muttering that cold was worse than prison, and that he would never fuck sheep again if he could only get warm.

"Don't worry, we can warm you right up," said Oz, yarding a butane lighter and a spray can of artificial whipping cream from his coat. He often carried a spray can of artificial whipping cream because its propellant was nitrous oxide, one of what he termed the Glorious Gasses, and which he could bleed from the container and inhale by holding its nozzle just so. Flick a lighter in front of the nozzle, and – presto! – he had a blowtorch that would melt a snowman. This he did, and with a whoosh the frost and all exposed stubble disappeared from the poor hitchhiker's face. An unexpected phenomenon also occurred: the car's windows were instantly covered with a fuzzy mat of frozen creamed nitro. Hot gas coalescing on cold glass can be messy.

"Jeez!" said Oz.

"I'm burning! Take me to the hospital! Please don't kill me!" cried our passenger.

He wasn't burning, but he was spooked. Beryl smeared clear a circle in the windshield and steered for St. Paul's, where our passenger jumped out and ran away before she came to a complete stop. We checked each other for burns or signs of chemical poisoning, breaking into relieved laughter when we decided we were okay. We had a horrible time cleaning gunk off the car, but returned it in spotless condition and full of gas that Oz bought. When he showed her his new driver's license, Wanda fed him a chocolate cake and said that she was proud of him.

He spent that night out celebrating while Beryl and I headed for the double bed that was available when he was gone. It was in the living room – the only other rooms were a kitchenette and a bathroom – wedged between the random mantelpiece and the building's one window.

We were at that delicious point in lovemaking where you are inside the Pearly Gates and lined up to meet God when the window popped open and Richie Darling started climbing through to join us. Richie was a sneaky but innocuous kid who was unsuccessfully majoring in English Literature, hiding in the shadows of other people's parties, peeping through other people's windows. I'll never know why he didn't just walk in through the front door, but I had a momentary flash of respect for his uncharacteristic aggressiveness.

Then I slammed the frame down on his head and told him to go away.

He flopped around like a trapped marten until I realized that of course he was stuck. I released him, shoved him back into the cold and rejoined God's receiving line.

Richie crunched through the snow to the closed and darkened campus athletic building, broke into the swimming complex and drowned himself in the 50-meter pool. His body was found in the morning.

Medicine Hat Turnaround

Charlie Pontefract invites me to drive to Canada with him. Still in a brace, feeling a mite blue for having killed Richie, I'm ready for a getaway.

It is March of '67, thirteen months since the Great Snowball Fight. Charlie and I have just finished a quick job as project assistants for a graduate student whose Master's thesis is supposed to document the premise that drug-using hippies are more susceptible than normal people to peer group pressure and subliminal prompts. When all his research and behavioral tests show that the opposite is true, he is told by his faculty advisors that he has obviously screwed up; he had better do something more scientific and useful if he wants an M.A. from the Treasure State. He will agree; will study the effects of interrupted fluorescent light on the appetites of white mice and become a successful psychologist working for California's Bureau of Pest Control. That is in the future. So is the fact that Charlie Pontefract is a father of my youngest daughter. Right now we're wheeling through a blizzard on our way to Calgary, Alberta. It's usually an easy day's drive from Missoula, but this weather is a trucker's nightmare. Good thing we're both speeded.

I like him. He's outrageous; plays guitar and sings in bars around the county. Over his bed he keeps a bullwhip that his girlfriend's parents think he uses on her all the time. He can deliver his patter in a variety of hilarious French, British and Bronx accents; may have dual US and Canadian citizenship, but who knows with Charlie.

We talk our way up Flathead Lake and across the Rockies. As we slither across the Highline east of Glacier Park my throat swells shut and hurts like hell. I have ignored the rules for proper amphetamine use and been volubly awake for 45 hours straight. I have smoked my first cigarettes. A carton of them. I am downright speechless.

Charlie smoothtalks us into Canada at Coutts. He tells the border guard that we're going to visit his father, who is an oil company engineer in Calgary. I never knew he had a father.

A few miles farther along we stop for gas at a crossroads; nearly miss the station for all the snow. The temperature is twenty below zero, pretty much like Missoula. We're both dopey now, get disoriented and drive east instead of north until I see a smiling 10,000-foot tall jackrabbit rising from the prairie whiteout.

"Look!" I croak. "A rabbit!"

He sees something different. Swears, then laughs. "Shit, it's Medicine Hat."

That two-mile high Bugs Bunny remains one of my most vivid hallucinations, but I am okay and Medicine Hat is the only town I ever mistake for a burrowing mammal.

Somehow Charlie finds the South Saskatchewan River and the new Trans-Canada Highway going northwest. Sucking in behind a semi, we make Calgary long after dark, driving beneath miles of mercury vapor lamps along Macleod Trail on our way to wake up some of his friends.

A few hundred yards away on Harley Road a moon-faced girl is fast asleep with a wiener under her pillow. She keeps one there to eat if she gets hungry in the night. She is seventeen years old. She is still waiting to be asked out on a date, but on solitary long walks has taught herself how to yodel. The wiener exudes a light funk that her family accepts without comment. They all like hot dogs.

The Moon-faced Girl

Years earlier the moon-faced girl with the strawberry imp's curl in the middle of her forehead is a toddler when she wakes up from her nap in a northern land. She stands up holding onto the railing of a child's crib. Her diaper is slipping down around her knees. She looks into her parents' bedroom and thinks *I am a baby, a baby in a crib.* She remembers this for her whole life.

The thought is so absurd, and the knowledge so incontrovertible, that she starts to laugh. *I am a baby! A baby in a crib! Oh, what could be sillier? And what will happen next?...*

...The moon-faced girl with the imp's curl in the middle of her forehead is eight years old and believes in the power of prayer.

She is walking to school when some bad boys from her class surround her. They tease her for the thick-lensed glasses her parents have bought for her to wear. She is far-sighted. The boys bump her and make fun of her red hair.

She closes her eyes and spins around, making a magic circle. She clasps her hands in front of her chest and prays for protection.

Friends come chattering up the street. The bad boys scatter like leaves in the wind of her magic circle.

She decides to become a nun...

...Becoming a nun is more difficult for the girl with the imp's curl than she thought it would be. To begin with, she learns that she is a Protestant.

Undeterred, she takes her skinny ten year-old legs to Sunday school where she is told that Christ rose from the dead; that we can all live forever in Him.

I know! I know! She happily tells the teacher and her class. *We all live lots of lives. I don't remember living in Him, but I do remember living in London, England! I got to be a maid! And then I was a pony! And I got to be a boy, like a pirate! And I talked in Chinese!* Her eyes open wider with each recollection.

She is eventually moved to the back of the room. There she effortlessly channels low-grade spirits while everybody else concentrates on Bible studies and how to find the one hard path to salvation.

Flower Power

No man shall be compelled to goe out of the limits of this plantation upon any offensive warres which this commonwealth or any of its friends or confederats shall voluntarily undertake.

The Liberties of the Massachusets Collonie in New England, 1641

Come spring, my fancies turned to thoughts of joining the Students for a Democratic Society, so I did. The precepts of the SDS were hard to argue against: racial equality, sexual equality, no war by presidential fiat. The FBI built dossiers on everybody who believed in such twaddle.

I tossed some clothes and a notebook into my guitar case and went to a San Francisco peace conference as a Rocky Mountain representative of SDS; slept on the floor of Rummel's spartan studio digs. Lyndon Johnson and Ho Chi Minh had also been invited to participate, but declined, being busy with the war and all. Hundreds of us shared anti-war tactics and strategies, passed resolutions, adopted manifestos, smoked dope, made love and gave hope to Southeast Asian communists that America would not go down fighting for colonial empire.

My contribution to the conference was small, confined to asking my fellow delegates if we should consider armed as well as passive resistance to a government that acted unconstitutionally. They said no, asked me where I was from, made eyes at each other when I said I was a Montanan – most of them were from the West Coast, the Northeast or Madison, Wisconsin. They were beautiful, devoted people willing to catch mild hell from their countrymen for speaking uncomfortable truths, yet – Lord love a duck – the women cried and the men fulminated indignantly for hours over the histories and plights of the downtrodden. While they acted with pure hearts and greater wisdom than the folks who waved the nearest bunting and chanted "My Country, Right or Wrong," I would have preferred spending more time riding around the city on the cable cars. One of the advantages of basing decisions on ethics, principles and logic ought to be that the debate is short and to the point, leaving lots of free time for everyone to gambol about as they await retribution.

A contingent from The Society of Friends told us it planned to sail a small boatload of medical supplies across the Pacific, through the Gulf of Tonkin and into the North Vietnamese port of Haiphong, where American bomber attacks were causing civilian casualties. Its organizers were asking for volunteers to crew the ship, so – having had some experience designing and sailing a dinghy on a freshwater pond – I signed on as an ordinary seaman. I admired the Quakers: without monopolizing the microphones at these confabs they were activist to the core.

Haight-Ashbury was the epicentre of youth culture that summer. The district was jammed day and night with piratical dealers and dopers, narcs, vendors, women in mini-skirts or flowing gowns, men in bell bottoms, tourist buses for those afraid to mingle; sandals were everywhere, the streets were full of feet and I was the only person wearing socks. There was so much hemp smoke in the air that you could get zonked, meet three saviours, five jugglers and a guru, contract the clap and have an existential experience just by going down the block to get takeout. Here was a gorgeous, steamy hole in the ice of the Cold War's geopolitics.

The district was fairly safe by Bay area standards, unlike Oakland or parts of the Embarcadero – where I was robbed at knife-point by a pair of junkies – or Fillmore. My final evening in San Francisco was spent in the Fillmore district, a lone white kid somewhat unwisely stoned on LSD, gawking around as a slack-water fog crept in. I suppose no one likes strangers loitering in the neighbourhood at midnight – I guess it was midnight; the junkies had ripped off my watch. The locals looked more menacing by the hour. There sure were a lot of black people living around here. I stopped to sit under a broken streetlight and listen to the sounds of the city: radio music; disembodied phony laughter; swearing; sirens. Except for the sirens and the fog, it was pretty much like a Livingston Saturday Night, only up on the Yellowstone a Chinese gang packing handguns wouldn't have appeared out of the mist to check me out, snort at my stupidity and escort me out of the place as they made their own escape after some kind of reprisal raid.

Come to think of it, that trip to California and back was extra weird. I might have been an SDS member, but I certainly wasn't on its payroll – if it ever had one. I hitched rides both ways.

On the way down, I met a hippie who thought we should jerk each other off like the ancient Greeks used to do. It was a harmless enough pastime in theory, but he smelled too much like me and had hair all over his face. Oh, well.

On the way back I was dropped off in Sparks, Nevada, and went into a café to buy lunch. A sheriff's deputy followed me, waited until I'd paid for a burger and pushed me out the door before it was served.

"Are you a peacenik?" he asked as he searched through my guitar case for drugs that were in my boots.

"Do you mean: is there a difference between right and wrong?" Redefining the question was a technique I had been taught in debate class. The deputy grabbed me by the shirt collar; said he hated smart-asses. I believed him. He gave me ten minutes to leave town.

Not wanting to enter lock-up with this guy, I gladly jumped into the first car that came by; found myself with a trio of nasty punks who decided to take me into the desert and beat my brains out. Luckily the driver was veering drunkenly all over the road and was stopped by a highway patrolman who recognized the situation right away. He turned me loose, but ordered the punks to stay in the car. If it is possible to furiously thumb a ride, that is what I did. I sped off toward Utah with a Mormon accountant as the patrolman very slowly wrote in his ticket book.

"Do you ever get lonely?" asked the man at the wheel. "I have money. Do you think I am attractive?"

Sweet Jesus.

As accountants go, he was a decent man: US Navy reservist; completed his Christian mission to some unpronounceable place in Brazil; married; five children so far; liked his job. He said that his curse was that of loving too much and too many. I said that sounded strange, coming from a Mormon.

He sighed, "My religion doesn't permit men to love men, or women to love women, like *that*."

"You can toss me out for saying this, but I have heard that your religion doesn't even permit you to drink coffee. Why not be a Unitarian?"

"Because I am a Mormon."

Isn't that the way.

I told him that, sadly, I had proved to myself that I was sexually attracted to only the female half of the human race, although he was darned handsome. He bought me dinner in Elko; handed me $20 when he dropped me off in Salt Lake City in the moonlight.

Salt Lake may have been a fine spot in which to be conceived, but it was a dead zone for hitchhikers – plenty of traffic but no rides until I'd walked through town and hours up the road to Ogden, passing two long-haired travelers asleep in a drainage ditch. They woke up long enough to ask in British accents for food. Tourists on a tight budget; said they had been trying for three days to get a ride out of here. Like any good Samaritan, I gave them candy bars and a dexamil. God approved, finally sending the silver Freightliner that rolled me to Anaconda, and the Flathead chief who carried me home in the front seat of his brand new Pontiac.

The war was going badly for America and its few allies. News correspondents were encouraged to publicize stories of villages being liberated from the Viet Cong, but the villages wouldn't stay liberated long enough for the film crews and reporters like Dickie Chapelle to get pictures without getting killed. General William Westmoreland was in charge of this growing American debacle, so he got creative and ordered the troops to forget liberation and go for body counts, real or fabricated. It didn't matter as long as there was a Performance Index to leverage more men and money from Congress.

Our armed forces weren't swamped with volunteers right then, and 25% of Missoula County's draftees were ignoring their orders to report for induction. I was feeling pretty useful and excited about sailing off with the Quakers, when a registered letter arrived from the U.S. State Department.

My passport had been cancelled. Somebody using the stamp of the Secretary of State also told me that I was hereby confined to the boundaries of the Lower 48: I could no longer dream of drilling for oil in Alaska or surfing in Hawaii, to say nothing of sailing through the Gulf of Tonkin with crates of bandages and penicillin.

There was more: I was ordered to report any change of address to federal authorities; all violations were punishable with a ten-year prison sentence.

This was nothing less than internal political exile, milder than what the Russian czarist regimes put their dissidents through, but the same hammer. The letter was careful to charge me with no crimes, for I had committed none. But a ban on Alaska and Hawaii? These people had gone stark raving mad.

Land of the free.

That wasn't my America anymore.

Of course it was the same land it had long been: an economic powerhouse, freer than most, once revolutionary but now a pillar of the status quo. It's funny how injustice is easier to bear if it's not directed at you.

As usual, I was certain about what I would do or not do under the circumstances.

I would not be put into a position where I had to kill or be killed by some poor guy who was fighting for his homeland.

I was going to continue to speak my mind as if I was a free man.

I would not let self-righteous goons ever put me in jail for doing so. I was clearly not cut from the same cloth as Eugene V. Debs or Big Bill Haywood or other great Americans who had been willing to be martyred to make the nation more worthy.

Canada was calling.

Canada: where Sitting Bull received asylum after daring to fight and beat the U.S. cavalry at Little Bighorn; where the Underground Railroad once smuggled escaped southern slaves to freedom; the Land O' Goshen that Chief Joseph and his Nez Perce tried but failed to reach; the land unknown to most Americans that is assumed to lie somewhere between Minnesota and the North Pole.

The SDS was also calling. Before I jumped ship, could I help organize a Montana contingent of supporters to march in a big anti-war parade being held in Seattle?

I sure could. And did. For the most part I am proud of my contribution to that demonstration, which involved more than 20,000 people. Too bad for The Cause that young Alex, one of the men I'd recruited, got his picture splashed across the front page of the *Seattle Times.* He was a Canadian Doukhobor, which was originally a pacifist Russian religious sect with roots going back to Leo Tolstoy. Thousands of them had moved to Canada around 1900, escaping internal exile like mine. Free for a while to live their dream they split into warring factions of true believers, sharing only a distrust of soldiers and secular government. Alex belonged to the Sons of Freedom sect. The organizing committee put him into the front ranks of the march, figuring to give some international cachet to the event.

Unknown to us until that day, whenever they especially wanted to impress God with their sincerity the Sons of Freedom would do so by standing stark naked before Him and the whole world.

I thought the front page *Times* photograph of Alex was well-composed; the organizers were certain it had destroyed the political message they had spent months crafting, and they rather unfairly held me responsible. I guess my name was struck from the rolls of the SDS because they never contacted me again.

I decided that my spine had healed enough that I could work to get some cash for my escape, but didn't make any bagging bread for an hour in the refrigeration locker of an industrial bakery – my fingers froze. And I didn't make much as a tree planter before getting fired for being too slow. I did better mopping up forest fires with a crew of Woody Street winos that always stank to high heaven until they sweated out the juice, but it wasn't full-time work, so I invested my bankroll in some housepainting equipment, went into business for myself, and was broke within a month. I didn't know the first thing about painting, and had underbid.

Selling my last textbooks for cash to buy an Amway retail samples kit, I became a door-to-door salesman for household cleaning products. The women of Missoula were much better dealers than I was, and relieved me of all my free samples in a single morning without buying so much as a box of soap.

I knew I was getting edgy when, on successive nights, I drank far too much of other people's beer; threw a good friend out a second-storey window; ran another's skull through a wall. These were harsh times, and a tendency toward violence is not a good sign in a bantamweight.

Myra was killed by a drunk driver while she was visiting her parents up on the highline near Havre. We all loved Myra. She was one of those doves who promises a gentler future. Busted and broken on a highway.

Enoch's spine was blown apart by his father, who shot his son in the back with that sweet 20-gauge during a domestic dispute. Enoch didn't like being kept alive in an iron lung, and was able to ask his girlfiend to shut it down when no one else was in the hospital room where he was confined.

They kissed while he died.

Quietly crying, she waited until she knew that nothing could ever bring her dire lover back to life, then plugged the machine back into its power socket and called for a nurse.

"Enoch has left the building," she said.

There Is a Godot

I was squatting in the dusty alley, very hungry and mindlessly watching flies crawl through the broken screen of the back door into the house when Lynn Baker showed up sporting a meticulously groomed goatee. Of all my pre-law friends, only he and a few others were still matriculating, but they were on summer holidays.

"Grab your guitar, Gary, and come with me. We're going to work on the railroad."

He had found jobs for the two of us on a Northern Pacific crew that was replacing track in the drylands near the Montana-North Dakota border.

The work was tough. Not only was I out of shape, but I'd lied about my weight in order to get hired. There was a weight requirement because my particular job was throwing heavy wooden ties off a flatbed car under a blistering sun. Halfway through the second day, I fainted and sailed off the railcar along with the tie I was tossing; didn't break any bones. The gang boss should have fired me for being inept, but he took pity and put me in charge of the water car, a little machine that ran along the tracks delivering water to the section crew. I replaced a guy who'd come to work drunk and had managed to chop off some fingers by running over them with the car. *He* was fired. The gang boss was an Italian gandy dancer with skin like leather, who worked like a horse all day and drank like a fish all night. I never understood more than a few words he said. Mostly, he would point and yell until you figured out what he wanted you to do, then he would go yell at somebody else. We all admired him the way you respect a drill sergeant. We slept in a company boxcar. We laid some good track, but it was boring, sad and ultimately revolting to be stuck at night in a boxcar full of men with salty armpits as they recounted their drunks, their whores and their cheating girlfriends.

The pay was good, and in a month I had made enough money to get out of the country. I said goodbye to Lynn, jumped off the work train as it was pulling a grade outside Dickinson, hitched a ride to Missoula, found Beryl, and was told that she fully intended to forego higher education and come north with me. We crossed the border into British Columbia and rented an apartment in Vancouver, an act that could get me a decade in McNeil Island federal penitentiary. In those days you could apply for Canadian citizenship from within the country, which is what I did.

Canada expelled me faster than you can say Bo Diddley. The immigration scoring matrix gave the interviewing official a substantial say in the applicant's final score; the interviewer judged my presence to be an ugly blot on the national landscape.

From a culinary perspective, it was disappointing to be expelled. While Vancouver's hamburgers weren't as greasy as I liked, I was going to miss the city's fish and chips. My pride was also hurt. I saw myself as desirable, morally upstanding and ambitious in a non-directed sort of way. Immigration Canada could not see much personal potential in me, yet I knew from personal experience that they were letting some real losers into the fold. According to their law, I could apply again in six months.

Thwarted but unfazed, Beryl and I rode the Greyhound to Seattle where she got a job as a telephone operator and I became a night-shift janitor at the University of Washington hospital. The rest of the crew consisted of a long-haired white dope dealer and twenty black guys for whom this was a second job that paid for the samba line of purple and pink second-hand Cadillacs that cruised the main entrance to pick them up from work every morning.

Our mission was to keep everything shiny and spotlessly clean. This required constant effort, so we emphasized shiny. The dealer and I were token whites on a veteran team, and I was easily accepted once I learned the house rule, which was that nobody could actually work except during the first and last hours of any shift, when you were to be seen furiously flying at it. Most of the men disappeared to sleep an hour into the shift, not to be seen again until dawn. It was easy to do – UW had more rooms and cubbyholes than Versailles, though the servants didn't raise chickens and milk cows on the top floor of UW. The dope dealer would sneak downtown to ply the trade for which this gig was merely a cover. I read a lot and hung out with a guy who had been there for years – long enough to have taught himself barrelhouse and gospel piano on an instrument somebody had donated to the place.

They all hated cleaning the morgue because it was full of cold, dead people. To me this was better than being in a room full of hot, dead people, so I frequently swamped out the morgue for them. Orderlies had cleaned the bodies that were stored there; all I had to do was to disinfect the floor and make sure no one had stuck chewing gum on the gurney before he died.

I did not squander my paid free time at the hospital.

I studied and got certified by the State of Washington to be a Floor Maintenance Engineer, which meant I could pour Dow chemicals across the surface of entire building wings, mop and vacuum them up, flush them into the public water system, then rewax without constant supervision.

Sometimes Beryl would come over in the middle of the night to sing soul music with the guys. She was a good singer and was welcomed by everyone. After jamming for a while, the two of us would slip away to Room 574B or an examination room with a nice view of Seattle's skyline.

I assiduously prepared for the ministry by reading Ambrose Bierce, Mark Twain, the Bible, pilgrim governor William Bradford's *History of the Plymouth Plantation*, Sun Tzu's *Art of War,* Aesop's *Fables*, *Discover Mecca*, *Buddha for Dummies* and *Rolling Stone* Magazine in the janitor's closet. In the spring I received my ordination papers from the Church of Universal Life. It cost me ten dollars, and I had to write a hundred word essay about God, mankind and the universe. Here it is:

Like turnips, we spend most of eternity being either unborn or dead. These are apparently God's preferred states for all matter. Think about it. This does not seem ideal. A minister's role is to help us to laugh, to cry and to refrain from killing each other prematurely during our brief sojourn on Earth. This calling is made difficult by the intimations that our lives have already been lived and that time is merely an artificial construct. Our fates are truly written on our foreheads, leaving us with the secret and sacred knowledge that, with a light heart, it is time to board the Titanic, enjoy her orchestra and hope to prove worthy as she sails forever west with her passengers on a maiden voyage that will certainly end in an accident.

Yes, I was now a reverend, if not reverent, and registered alongside Oral Roberts by the State of California. Ironically, Universal Life was established by a vacuum cleaner salesman attempting to force the state to tax the fly-by-night churches that were being founded by used car dealers looking for bigger markets and more generous personal income deductions. What he got was the financial and legal support of nearly every religious institution in the nation, because if the courts declared him to be bogus, so were they. They didn't want to be bogus. Credentials are important if you are soliciting as God's representative.

Suffice it to say, the Church of Universal Life was quickly brought under the panoply of the world's other great religions. When I despair of holy fundamentalists ever putting aside their differences in the interest of a Greater Good, I fondly recall how quickly they did so in the case of yet another of God's disciples, a simple vacuum cleaner salesman.

I didn't use my ministerial status to avoid active military service. As a matter of fact, I contacted the office of the US Joint Chiefs of Staff, offering to enlist if (a) we first changed sides in Vietnam, or (b) I was appointed to supersede General Westmoreland.

Not expecting an immediate reply, I got ready for a second assault on Canada. This time I would skip work, bop over to Missoula and bring in the heavy artillery: Professor David Ludniska, Doctor of Psychiatry. We had first been introduced to each other by a mutual bedmate. David was tenured at the university, so he was outspoken and truckled to no one. This was good for him, because he was not normal. He never wanted to be an academic. After earning his Ph.D. from Princeton he had started a private practice in Connecticut that achieved remarkable results, yet had to close within a year due to lack of clients.

The beauty – and the problem – of his clinical approach, as he explained it to me, was in his billing system. He charged no hourly rate. Instead, when you had a session with him, the deal was that you had to cough up $100 on the spot whenever he tapped the small bronze bell on his desk. He tapped it whenever he thought you weren't being honest with yourself in what you were saying. Patients with ordinary incomes usually declared themselves cured in a single visit; wealthier clientele tended to hide their issues about $2000 longer, although David said it was surprising how concerned with cost the rich could be.

Word soon hit the street that there was a shrink who didn't think your neuroses were personally intriguing or complicated or hard to solve, and business tanked.

One day, Hartford; next day, heartbreak. Such can be the path of spiritual pioneers.

He was a natural pacifist and activist who promoted personal and political honesty. Talk about setting high goals. Over the years he had built an international network of professional peers who shared these views. In a pinch, David could call on his associates in Canada and Sweden to offer particular American draft dodgers a job in their country in order to help them immigrate. I'd sent several candidates to him; he would always help if you didn't try to bullshit him.

I knew I would find him in his campus office over lunch hour, eating kosher dill pickle and cranberry sandwiches and enjoying the blatant sexual advances of a chorus line of co-eds who queued up to seek his advice, perform fellatio, and schedule later liaisons.

"I need help, David."

"Don't we all!"

"I need a job."

"Sure. I know a grad student who is looking for somebody to do sleep deprivation experiments on. Two weeks or so. Money's not much, but meals are provided because you have to stay in an observation room."

"I need a job in Canada."

His eyes went opaque for an instant as he rummaged through his brain looking for Canada. "Sure, I can help you. Speak French?"

"Nyet."

"So much for Quebec. My British Columbia contacts are maxed out. Nova Scotia is on sabbatical. Alberta is under faculty review for hiring too many temp assistants already. Do you want Saskatchewan or Ontario?"

I chose Ontario. Saskatchewan was hard to pronounce.

Not long afterwards, I received a formal letter from the Dean of Psychology at the University of Western Ontario: he needed me; the Dominion needed me; only someone with my special academic credentials and experience could fill a new staff position. Taken to the right border crossing, a legitimate offer of employment scored you major points with the immigration officials. That letter was not an invitation to exile; it was my ticket out of a claustrophobic superpower; my ticket home.

Thank you, Dean. And thank you, David.

Sign of the Dog

The rhododendrons were blooming in Seattle when I quit my job and bought a '57 Chev to take north – really to take east and south, because the part of Canada to which I was headed lies in what Montanans consider to be the "banana belt" between Detroit, Michigan and Buffalo, New York. Although it was farther to drive, my plan was to replay Chief Joseph's run for freedom from Missoula straight up to Alberta, then east. If worse came to worse and I failed to get landed immigrant status at the border, Charlie Pontefract – who was also worried about being drafted – developed a fallback strategy for us both: we would hike the Rockies into Canada, buy fake IDs and wait for the war to blow over. Charlie loved an adventure, and was full of good ideas like that. Fortunately, I was left to my own devices when he called from Calgary to tell me that he had gone there to visit his godmother and been denied entry back into the US because he was Canadian, not American. I hadn't known that. Apparently neither had he.

I didn't ask Beryl to come with me; she volunteered. She was that kind of person. She said that she would keep punching switchboards in the Emerald City until I got settled.

We took a few weekend trips together before I left: one to see her family; another to say goodbye to mine. With the Wrights, blood was never much thicker than water, but I really wanted to hug Fay and Ken again. Beryl's folks joined us and everyone got along well. Dad was different from the man who had locked me up a year ago, and gave me $500 to "help out up there." He mused about the similar responsibilities of teachers and parents to raise their children/pupils to fit into the world around them, and – failing that – to make sure they were tough enough to endure as oddballs. I felt like I'd passed an arcane test. I guess my brother had too: Ken confidentially told me that he had slammed Dad to the floor during a whiskey-fueled argument; that life with father had been better since. Ken was fourteen.

Beryl and I plucked Oz out of Missoula and brought him back to Seattle for a visit. On the return trip, they both wanted to see Grand Coulee dam, which required a short detour. I was driving, speeded on amphetamines, and was not going to stop for anybody's dam, so they slipped me a tranquilizer. I remember growing unaccountably drowsy and asking Beryl to take the wheel. I woke up after dark in the back seat. Looking bleary-eyed through the rear window, I saw them cavorting in the multi-coloured lights that shone on the mighty Columbia as it poured over the spillways of the Grand Coulee. Friends.

My last hours in the Land of Liberty were a microcosm of the past two lunatic years.

Oz had talked me into letting him drive Beryl back to the coast in the Chevy. That was on a Sunday. I was going to leave the country on Tuesday. At noon Monday he called me at Marybeth's. As was the social custom at the time, she and I had dropped acid and were nakedly exploring our shared universe prior to a going-away party scheduled for later. It was a wrench to hear his disembodied voice telling me that there might be a slight delay in his return: he was in jail in Seattle.

"Where's my car?" I've always had a fine sense of priorities, even stoned.

"It's safe, but I am in jail. I can't remember Beryl's phone number. This is my one call. Could you get her to come down and bail me out?"

"Where is my car?"

"It's impounded somewhere. The police – they've been pretty good about the whole thing – took it away when they arrested me."

"Arrested you for what?"

"Going the wrong direction on the Alaska Way Viaduct."

Leave it to Oz. What a cruddy driver.

"You're at the station now?" I wanted to be sure.

"Yeah. That's part of being arrested. Sorry."

I loved Oz, everyone did, but I was mad.

"Let me talk to someone there," I said. It was hard to concentrate with Marybeth slithering around my body, her hands driving me crazy. Oooo.

A duty officer came on the line. I told him I was the vehicle owner.

"Your friend says he was operating the vehicle with your permission. Is that right?" he asked.

"If I say yes, will you give him back my car?"

"Your vehicle has been impounded, sir. We can only release it to the registered owner, after you pay impound fees."

"Fuck!" I exclaimed. A rocketful of chromosomes had just exploded on the launch pad. The atmosphere rained a jubilation choir of motherless children. Marybeth, who bore responsibility for this, cooed as she greased us both with orphans.

"What did you say, sir? Was the vehicle being operated with your permission?" he repeated.

I was screwed up. I looked at Marybeth. No, I *had* been screwed, sort of. This was screwy. The interpretations of the word brought on paroxysms of mirth. It was extremely good acid. *Get a grip. There is a cop on the line.*

"My car was stolen, officer. I don't know the man you're holding. Please keep him in jail until I can get over there. It might take a while." And I hung up.

I filled Marybeth in on the gist of the phone call, which sent us into hysterical giggles for an hour before we called Beryl and asked her to please get Oz out of the clink. I would reimburse her the money as soon as I could find a ride over there. "Oh, that Oz!" she said tolerantly. She also told me that a letter addressed to me from the government had just arrived. Should she open it? I said yes; perhaps it was offering me command of the U.S. army. Nope. It was an order to report for induction.

Some of the steam went out of the farewell party when people learned that I didn't have a car in which to leave. Folks were nice; Bitterroot Al and his gal Sal brought gallons of wine and buckets of beer, but I felt like a dork. Cynthia Schuster, that doyen of philosophers, slipped another five hundred dollars into my jeans, along with an observation that Thomas Hobbes – my favorite Great Thinker – was, in her estimation, more of a politician than true *philosophe*. Barclay Kuhn overheard her and soon the two of them were nattering and swinging their arms around for emphasis as they debated the value of pure reason in human affairs. Someone's randy German shepherd came on my pants leg when I wasn't watching. That seemed insulting when you considered that I was born in the Year of the Dog in Chinese cosmology. You would think your propitious animal would show more respect. Poor Linda Hopkins overdosed on something – her boyfriend had dumped her – so a bunch of us held her up by the armpits and walked her around town for a couple of hours to keep her awake and breathing. Afterwards the rescue team packed into Eddy's Club to eat peanuts and swill more Great Falls Select until closing time. It had turned out to be a decent evening.

Marybeth and I weaved back to her place around two in the morning. My Chevy was parked at the front door. A beaming Oz met us inside. We never locked our doors.

"You are supposed to be in jail," I said. "I told the cops you stole my car. How did you get loose?"

"You left me with no choice but to talk my way out," he grinned.

It seems that the station cop had garnered much more information from our phone call than I gave him credit for. He told Oz that his friend sounded high on drugs and was trying to play a joke on him. Oz agreed that I had a severe addiction problem. He also told the officer that in Missoula there were no weird on-ramps and banks of flashing lights like the ones that had sent him the wrong way down the viaduct; that he was a country boy who found himself momentarily discombobulated in the big city. Leave it to Oz. The cop let him free; he was walking out of the police station as Beryl was walking in with bail money. They went to the impound yard and together convinced the attendant to release the car. He told me that Beryl sent her love, and proudly added that he had just completed the eight-hour trip from the coast without a single collision.

Sometime after sunrise Marybeth kissed me goodbye. At peace with my world, I rumbled out of the United States of America. I have not been greatly missed.

Can't you hear them guitars skankin'?

Lucky Dube

The Book of Bands

Otto and Otto

Otto and Otto were Customs and Immigration officials, the entire and unarmed complement of border guards on duty at the Alberta entry point. They were halfway through their bratwurst lunches when I drove into the customs bay and applied for Canadian citizenship.

They couldn't have been more helpful. After introducing themselves, they took turns eating and helping me complete the application forms. They smiled when they read the dean's employment offer.

"This is good," said Otto.

"Very good," agreed Otto. "We must now ask if you have sufficient money to support yourself until you become established in, uh, Ontario."

I plunked down the travelers' cheques and wad of bills from Dad and Cynthia Schuster; it seemed like big bucks in my pocket, but looked pathetic lying on the customs counter. At least it was my own money and not an "immigration packet" like the kind our underground would supply to dodgers, and which they were asked to return via a Canadian contact so that it could be recycled.

Otto and Otto exchanged glances.

"Quite sufficient," they said.

I braced myself for the "personal interview" that would come next, and which had blown me out of the water and out of the country last autumn. It never happened. Instead, I saw Otto write "50 points" on the checklist he was keeping. That was the most an applicant could score on the interview section. He totaled my points and showed the result to his partner, who nodded in approval.

"Welcome to Canada, Mr. Wright," said Otto.

"Now let us talk about Nazis," said the other Otto.

And he meant it, so we did. Their official duties concluded, the border agents felt free to talk informally. I learned that Otto Weismann and Otto Adler were both sons of immigrant parents who had fled to Canada from Germany in 1938. Unadulterated kismet had brought them together at this crossing. Neither of them liked Nazis, Italian fascists, Soviet or Chinese communists, Spanish royalists, tinpot dictators or American imperialists. Insomuch as it lay within their power to do so, they were aiding and abetting anyone who was in trouble for twisting a lion's tail. How much my own efforts and preparation had to do with becoming a landed immigrant – the first step to citizenship – was made evident as I shook hands and prepared to drive away.

"Have a good time in Vancouver," said Otto.

"Be sure and return the money so someone else may show it to us," said Otto.

O Canada

It was a long haul across the prairies to Lake Superior, Lake Huron and Ontario. I loved the trip. I was at liberty to do anything I wanted with the rest of my life. I had escaped from Devil's Island. It was a wonderful feeling. It still is.

The Chevy's transmission dropped out onto Dundas Street in the exact centre of London. Immigrants could not sell their foreign-registered cars for 90 days after entering the country and I had neither the money nor the inclination to repair the Chev. Some people helped me push it out of the traffic. I left the keys in the ignition, picked up my guitar, briefcase and box of worldly possessions and walked off towards the UWO campus. Along the Thames River (yeah, like the English Thames) on Ridout Street I got tired of carrying everything, saw a Suite For Rent sign and moved into an apartment in an old 1880s stone manse full of raccoons.

My university research duties consisted of writing one-sentence employment preference descriptions for what would be a new national job aptitude test. The old one was based on cultural stereotypes (e.g. *Would you rather listen to an opera, drink beer, or play with kittens? Would you rather save the world, save your soul, or Undecided?*). The new one would be honest and straightforward. For instance, if you answered "yes" to *I would like to open other peoples' mail and crush cardboard boxes all day*, you would get two points as a Filing Clerk or Postal Employee. Saying "yes" to *I would like to cut down big trees with my Stihl chainsaw* would indicate a preference for logging. *I like making financial deals with someone else's money – as long as I am not personally liable for losing it* would get you Banker or Corporate Chairman points.

Several of us were hired to write these lines. We shared a cubbyhole office; had a weekly quota of sentences to submit to the dean. He wouldn't accept more than our quota from any of us, to keep the content from becoming stylized, so I talked him into letting me work from home and leave more office space for the others. I could finish a week's quota in half a day, leaving plenty of time to produce some unmarketable inferior fiction. I still have most of it filed away; the tastes of the reading public change; perhaps they will someday hit rock bottom and I will find a publisher.

Lack of unwarranted immediate literary renown was the only fly in my ointment. Ottawa confirmed my status in May. In five years I would be eligible to become a fully-fledged Canadian if I had stayed out of jail and off the welfare rolls. After that I could go to jail or go on welfare as often as I wanted. I typed and signed a scurrilous letter to the U.S. State Department (copy to President Lyndon Baines Johnson) renouncing my citizenship. That would leave me stateless, but what the hell. As Benjamin Franklin said, "Those who would trade liberty for security deserve neither." The sun smiled down and the sap rose in the oak trees along Ridout Street as I whistled to the corner and flipped the letter into the big red mailbox.

Beryl flew out from Seattle in June. The crazy woman had turned down an invitation to sail to the South Pacific in the arms of a very nice investment broker, preferring to share what Americans were taught to believe would be a lifetime of pointless and brooding exile. To buy a second-hand van and make ends meet, I got a second job as a child care worker at Madame Vanier's centre for emotionally disturbed kids. Madame Vanier was the wife of one of the country's Governors General, who gave her imprimatur to the operations of this fine little institution.

Beryl married me in August. She had to - her visitor's visa was expiring. One of our necessary witnesses got sick an hour before the civil service, but we found a substitute on our way to the courthouse – a guy wearing a medieval jester's costume who had fallen asleep or overdosed in a Volkswagen Beetle nudged alongside an expired parking meter. We laughed and banged on the car window until he woke up, then asked him to attend our wedding. He smelled like stale hashish, but he was game. Our other witness was Mary, an older and very understanding Ontarian who came dressed in the *de rigeur* Eaton's pink satin woman's business day suit. Mary even thought to bring a camera, which showed more forethought than we brought to the occasion. Somewhere there is a picture of two newlyweds, a bleary-eyed clown and somebody's mother waving from the steps of the Middlesex Courthouse to a camera operated by a passing pedestrian.

Sparing no expense, I fed the Beetle's meter and treated everyone to breakfast at a downtown waffle house before walking home with Beryl on our honeymoon.

Compared to the Rockies, summer in the east was unrelievedly muggy, with five or maybe a dozen Londoners dying from lightning strikes each week during the afternoon thunderstorms. It was a short drive to Lake Erie, but in the '60s the lake was full of rotting dead fish that slapped you in the face when you went swimming and which littered the beaches when you slithered back ashore covered with fish slime and industrial pollutants from Detroit, Windsor, Toledo and Cleveland. I'm told that the lake has now been restored and is drawing vacationers from across the continent to the shores of those wondrous cities.

The staff of Madame Vanier's took me under its members' collective wing and introduced me to *their* Canada. This involved chugging gallons of Labatt's 50 ale after every shift, religiously watching Hockey Night in Canada, learning to call napkins *serviettes*, feeling safe with Canadian money because it's colour-coded in case you forget how to read numbers, grasping the communistic concept of equal health care for anyone in need, and always phoning a week ahead of time to let others know you're going to drop by for coffee. They were wonderful people raising healthy, well-adjusted families. They were sensitive to others. They held regular neighbourhood (not *neighborhood*) barbecues on their porch decks in the fug of summer or the icy snow of the Great Lakes winters. Because Canada is officially a bilingual nation, they had all studied enough French (not the native Quebec patois) in school to allow them to read the listed ingredients on cereal boxes in either language.

Such normalcy could have mentally unhinged Beryl and me if we hadn't met Paul and Angel. Paul was a tall, darkly handsome young drug dealer. Angel was his sloe-eyed tattooed girlfriend. He was charming and gregarious. She carried the pistol and watched his back. They had an apartment in the Victorian brownstone next door.

Paul was a retailer: he sold speed. Kilos and kilos of it. He always stashed his crystal in our side garden, to give him plausible deniability if he ever got pinched by the cops. I wouldn't be at particular risk since the stuff would be outdoors; could have been hidden by anybody. Paul said to help myself to all I wanted for my personal use. It was a simple and honourable time.

Oz visited us on his way to Istanbul. He had quit college and opened an import store in Missoula. His plan was to find strange things from all over the world, then sell them to Montanans.

The three of us dropped acid and Oz tried to drive us to Lake Huron. He got stopped twice for traffic infractions but played the Visiting American card to talk his way out of getting fined. After that we wouldn't let him drive anymore. Reaching the Bruce Peninsula at sunset we swam west into a placid copper Huron sunset. It's the only time in my life I have been in the water for more than three minutes without turning blue and sinking. On another day he and I took Beryl to Niagara Falls for her honeymoon.

Oz had found a "source" for a discount travel package to Turkey. It had him flying from Toronto to Athens and riding trains into Istanbul. Before we took him to the airport, he asked Beryl to give him a quick Tarot reading, "just for fun." He drew The Fool. Beryl told him to get serious and try again. He drew The Tower – a card full of broken people falling from the walls of a burning castle. Bad omen. A few weeks later we got a letter from him. He was ripped on LSD on a train somewhere in Macedonia, worried that the conductor would find his rail pass to be as fraudulent as his plane tickets had turned out to be. The letter was postmarked from Turkey, so we knew that Oz had managed to brazen his way out of another scrape.

1968. Forget Woodstock. While I became proficient at grabbing volatile pre-teens before they could stab somebody with a dinner fork, in the United States some sonuvabitch white cracker killed Martin Luther King.

Sirhan Sirhan put a bullet into Bobby Kennedy's brain; more into the crowd around him. The road to the presidency had been paved for Richard Milhaus Nixon – a blunt message to anybody else who might get uppity in America.

In times of loss and grief, oppressed people like to say that you can't kill an idea. Maybe not, but you sure as hell can stall the Cosmic Inevitable by shooting anyone in a position to make the idea a reality. Remember the Chicago Convention? America's moral compass, compromised at best, was blown to pieces in 1968.

Corky Evans married a young political activist named Bonnie, and they started packing to come north to where good people might make a difference. His father left too; Corky and his dad were never to meet again.

1968 was also a rare violent year in Canada. A Quebec separatist group called the FLQ kidnapped and murdered a British diplomat while he was in that francophone province. Pierre Trudeau, the country's recently elected Prime Minister, was still an unknown quantity whose political power base was in Quebec. He surprised everyone when he declared a national State of Emergency and called in the army. The FLQ was destroyed as an effective terrorist organization. Quebecois would continue to seek autonomy, but they would do so at the ballot box.

While North America went on a killing spree, I heeded Voltaire's Candide and tended to my own garden, as befits a stateless person. Autumn is kind to southern Ontario. Beryl and I took long walks in misty woods; held hands along the river.

A Mountie and a pair of FBI agents showed up at our house. I guess it was a routine followup; kind of late and low priority, but with 100,000 draft dodgers and antiwar activists now in Canada, they were busy. I hoped J. Edgar Hoover and the Bureau were spending as much time tailing Babe Rebozo as they were on keeping track of me.

I thought I was prepared for anything they could ask; didn't think I could stand waterboarding, but sodium pentothal or sleep deprivation held no special terrors. The agents had only one question.

"Are you being held here against your will?"

"Am I *what?*"

I was flabbergasted. Beryl laughed so hard that she had to leave the room to compose herself.

"Are you being kept here against your will? We're here to assure your safe passage back to the United States." The agents looked at the Mountie for confirmation. The stone-faced constable nodded.

Winter came. Snow and ice. With a mixture of 24-hour care, love, psychoanalysis, prescription drugs and behavioural modification therapy, Madame Vanier's children made steady and predictable progress towards normalcy.

One of the indicators of that respectable though banal state of mind is the ability to work with others to accomplish a task. This was something most of our kids couldn't do when they arrived at the institute. That's why we staffers felt so good the night of the Maple Leafs Cockup, as it came to be known.

Chuck, my shift supervisor, got permission to drive a dozen of our more functional kids to Toronto to attend a Maple Leafs hockey game. A kind donor gave us tickets for his corporate box. We left London with no time to spare, and traffic was slow on the blizzard-bound 401. We were going to miss the opening faceoff.

"Everybody hold on!" Chuck barked, booting the gas pedal.

The kids, especially one called Jimmy, loved the sudden rush. Jimmy was dynamite-smart, with a very short fuse. With Chuck humming the national anthem, we passed a lot of vehicles; it was hard to tell how many because we could only see snow out the windows of the passenger van.

It wasn't long before a highway patrol car was on our rear bumper, siren on, lights flashing. That was good driving; he had to have been snow blind during the pursuit. Chuck pulled over to a stop. He was in serious trouble. Madame Vanier's always said that its children's safety came first.

Chuck wasn't much older than I was, but had much more experience as both a child care worker and a speeding driver. As the patrolman zipped up his parka and walked to the van, Chuck turned in his seat to face us all.

"Listen up, everybody! We're all in deep shit unless you do what Jimmy does. Got it?" Everybody nodded, including me. We all understood deep shit. "Okay, then. Jimmy, do your thing!"

He looked straight into the boy's eyes, then poked him in the sternum with his forefinger.

Jimmy hated being poked in the sternum. His father had done that as a precursor to vicious beatings.

Jimmy smiled and went berserk, lashing out at everything within reach. My glasses flew off. All the kids started screaming, jumping around, laughing or crying. I clamped onto Jimmy to keep him from hurting himself or somebody else. Little Charlene leapt like a monkey onto Chuck's back, yanking away at his hair. General pandemonium.

Chuck rolled down his window and turned to the patrolman.

"Hi, officer. We have a *situation* here."

We never made it to the game. Chuck didn't get a ticket or lose his job, though I never saw him driving children around again. We got a police escort back to London. The kids eventually settled down, pretty pleased with themselves. Jimmy was a hero, and each individual had a "success experience" working cooperatively as a unit. I had to get a new pair of glasses. After their baths, we let them all stay up late to watch the end of the game on television. Jimmy plunked himself alongside Chuck, falling asleep as the Maple Leafs lost to Chicago's Blackhawks in a 6-1 stinker.

Girl from the North Country

Southern Ontario has fine lightning storms and a good collection of Simcoe elms, but living there a year was enough for Beryl and me. We missed the mountains. The two of us headed for Vancouver in the summer of '69, soon after Paul died from a drug overdose that left Angel inconsolable.

Paul had not been in particular trouble with the mob, the cops or his clients. Sure, there was the time the mob threatened to kill him if he didn't ante up on a $10,000 note within 24 hours; but that minor glitch in their established working relationship had been smoothed over when it was discovered that a teller at the Bank of Nova Scotia had errantly transferred Paul's payment to a lucky recipient living across town. The mob boss had sent him a dozen roses and an apology as soon as the error was rectified.

Angel held a wake for Paul in her living room. We sat in a circle with seven or eight other people underneath a glittering disco ball that had been Paul's pride and joy.

No one spoke.

We joined hands and remembered him. As we did so, the ball, which hung suspended from the ceiling, began to swing. It traced a small arc like a pendulum; then it changed its mind and began circling on its restraining wire. The circles grew larger and faster. We stared upwards. Now it was whizzing around the room.

The wire hummed, then snapped with a bang. The globe of mirrors smashed against the wall, spraying the room with glass. Psychokinesis? Paul saying goodbye? Angel asked us to leave her lying among the shards, but we couldn't.

Group Therapy

The drive west with Beryl was more fun than the drive east without her the year before. We took a charming 1920s era ferry from the Bruce Peninsula, past the Flowerpot Islands, across the mouth of Lake Huron's Georgian Bay to Manitoulin Island and back to the north shore. We chased summer storms across the prairie provinces, tracking as many as seven concurrent thunderheads to the horizon as they dumped hail across otherwise sunny wheatlands studded with antelope. The Rocky Mountains and Lake Louise were postcard perfect; we picked sage along the Thompson River; cruised through the Fraser Canyon and glided into Vancouver smelling like fresh spice.

With a good reference from Madame Vanier's it didn't take long to get a job at Southside Mission as shift supervisor at a group home for emotionally disturbed teenage boys. I learned that it takes an expert to distinguish emotionally disturbed teenagers from typical ones. Michael Brewster, my boss, was only 26. He was from Michigan, and – like me – had come north to avoid the draft and do something worthwhile with his life. Half the staff was from the United States. Within a few months of my arrival it included Charlie Pontefract, also incarnated as a child care worker.

Michael and his wife Julie invited Beryl and me to move in with them and their incredibly stupid and playful large dog named Wagstaff. Michael and Julie loved Wagstaff. This was incomprehensible to me, but Julie was smart, petite, had long ashe-blonde hair and spoke in a contralto that drove men wild. I quickly found good things to say about their dog: the way he could run between your legs, trip you, steal the ball and puncture it whenever we played flag football in the park; how he liked to leap through the glass of the upstairs window to join us in the backyard for a barbecue; the spontaneity that caused him to jump from a moving car to try to catch a Frisbee that he saw some kids tossing to each other; the day he crawled into bed and onto *my* belly to give up his holy ghost.

Michael groomed me for success, but it eventually became obvious that helping others was not my *métier.* Unlike Madame Vanier's, physically restraining the kids was frowned upon. That meant I had to be more quick-witted than my charges, and I wasn't. When I took them to Vancouver Island for a team-building outdoors experience, they went snaky in their pup tents during an inconsequential coastal gale and threatened to walk off and hitch rides to the nearest city. Exasperated, I told them why their plan was not good but that it was their life to foul up if they wanted. They wanted. The Victoria police were picking them up and returning them to SM for a week afterwards.

Michael thought I might work more effectively with adults, so he made me one of the Mission's marriage counselors. I only had one couple for clients, a pair of querulous 50 year-olds foisted onto me by the senior counsellor.

They were not happy to have been passed off to a baby-faced twerp who wore round glasses and whose voice sounded like it was still breaking. I held no cachet for them.

They alternately bored me and drove me to distraction. A month into our sessions I recommended that they get divorced and split their cash and possessions equally among themselves and their lawyers.

"Life is too short to spend it with someone you don't want to kiss," I said.

While this is true, it is not what they wanted to hear.

They complained loudly, working in harness like the two old oxen they were. Their file was transferred to a more experienced and competent colleague who agreed with them that better interpersonal communications could salvage their marriage. They got to actively dislike one another for a further five years before moving on to three years of ugly divorce proceedings that resulted in them splitting their cash and possession equally among themselves and their lawyers.

"Maybe you're beyond regular social work," Michael said. I think I had become a "project" for him. He rarely gave up on his people; that is probably one of the reasons he was so good at his job.

He subcontracted Charlie and me to help him lead Encounter Group therapy sessions under the auspices of the Frikkin Island Self-Awareness Foundation. The foundation was the brainchild of Arthur Holmes, another of those Doctors of Psychology. Arthur – he told everyone to call him by his first name, but scowled if you called him Art – was a tall, salt-and-pepper bearded prophet in the emerging field of Personal Growth and Human Awareness. I never fully understood what the hell that meant spiritually, but I can tell you what it meant in practical terms.

Arthur first incorporated himself, a sure sign that someone is up to no good. Next, he made the down payment on 140 undeveloped acres of Frikkin Island, including a half mile of shell beach fronting Georgia Strait. His plan was to pay for the property by hosting high-class personal growth retreats for people who had American Express credit cards. Back then it was a sign of distinction to have American Express.

His problem was that the property didn't have even an outhouse on it; it was virgin. How could you get anybody to pay $600 for a weekend on an island that didn't have a shitter? By advertising to Americans from Seattle, San Francisco and Los Angeles, of course. *Come to Frikkin Island; help build a paradise with Dr. Arthur Holmes. Join the family. Learn to work with your hands and your hearts to grow as a human being and make the world a better place.*

The ads were expensive, but Arthur more than recovered the money he'd laid out as people flocked to Frikkin to become better humans. Michael, Charlie and I had missed the first couple of years, when clients paid to sleep under cedar bough shelters and dig latrines.

The new Main Lodge was open when we arrived on the tiny Frikkin ferry that shuttled between the island and Campbell River. The lodge was a magnificent piece of architecture, designed with lots of glass, peeled logs and native stone chimneys. The kitchen and meeting spaces on the ground floor were decorated and made more intimate with indoor arbutus trees and ferns in gigantic clay pots that had been hand-fired in a wood kiln by artistic volunteers. A wide maple staircase led to the second floor where Arthur and his wife had private quarters with bevelled bay windows overlooking the beach.

Our job was to lead afternoon encounter workshops that would help the two dozen paying customers – called "the family" – to jettison some psychic garbage, show honest emotion and get a short respite from hauling rocks, building cabins, digging a new well, gardening, delousing the chickens, chopping wood, preparing meals and washing dishes for all of us. After six hours of backbreaking labor, with another four to follow, it is no wonder that the "family" members loved to sit on cushions and talk about their inner demons and hangups for a while. We furnished pillows for people to scream at or hit if they wanted to express how mad they were at their parents; we encouraged them to take turns being the audience and star of a group soap opera; there was fruit juice; in the evenings there was alcohol and the chance to have sex with someone whose last name you didn't know. In my world these were all things any good friend would give you for free. Essentially, we were hiring out as Friends for the Weekend: a hybrid New Age escort agency.

Charlie was in his element, leading an advertising executive to a spectacular emotional breakthrough, going to bed with his wife, and receiving huge hugs from them both as they caught the ferry out. Michael, ever the professional, bedded a foxy young woman who was seeking support as she struggled to express her latent sexuality.

Unlike them, I had helped no one, and told Michael that it was time for me to move on. He agreed and said with every appearance of sincerity that South Side Mission would not be the same without me.

The Ballad of Jumbo Jefferson

He weighed eleven pounds at birth, so they named him Jumbo.

His father made eye-catching useless accessories for televisions, which were all black-and-white at the time. His most successful gizmo was a thin sheet of rainbow-tinted plastic that people could press onto their screens to make "Technicolour TV."

Nobody remembers what Jumbo looked like as a kid. His parents didn't take family photographs or buy his annual school pictures, so it was fun for the plastic surgeon to rebuild his face when he was almost killed in a traffic accident at the age of fourteen. The doctor was a Cary Grant movie fan, and Jumbo came out of each successive surgery looking more and more like Cary Grant, only with a taunting Billy the Kid lip. His father didn't like Cary Grant and called a halt to the facial reconstruction before Billy the Kid could be fully integrated into his face. Five years later it was the first feature Michael and I noticed when we met him at the messy offices of the *Georgia Straight*, Vancouver's alternative press newspaper.

He wore a seersucker suit and walked with a cane and a limp. He was just one of the young men who had entered the country posing as a member of the Seattle United Church Devotional Chorale. The chorale frequently bused up from the States to give open air concerts sponsored by various Vancouver churches. It always went home with fewer members than it arrived with. The *Straight* served as a clearing house, finding accommodation, food and even lawyers for the new arrivals. Jumbo was going to stay with Michael, Julie, Beryl and me until he found his footing.

The kid was an army deserter, not a dodger. His issues were not with America; they were universal: he disliked authority and he had a sense of humour. He wanted to be a medic but Basic Training had shown him to be a crack shot, so he was selected to become a sniper. Training for that involved crawling through a fake southern California jungle which had been prepared with life-size Viet Cong targets that would pop from behind trees or out of the ground. Using single-fire only, he was supposed to shoot the Cong as they appeared. He did it with ease, only to be ordered to crawl through the swamp and the weeds again, for practice. This time he amused himself by blasting all the Cong in the head instead of the body because it was a greater challenge. His drill instructor had told him to always go for body shots; he wasn't training show-offs. He ordered Jumbo to do the course a third time.

"Body shots only, dickhead," said the DI.

"Yes, SIR," replied Jumbo, flipping his rifle onto full automatic.

Statistics from the war show that it cost around a million dollars to kill a Viet Cong, somewhat less to strafe an innocent civilian. At $5000 apiece, the automated targets upon which Jumbo practiced were cheaper than the real thing but twenty of them still amounted to a lot of loose change. The servo-motors that drove them were mounted on the targets themselves. The odds of destroying the motor with a single shot were acceptable to the army ordnance department. An accurate and tightly grouped burst of automatic fire was another story.

"Die, Ho Chi Minh!" yelled Jumbo as he charged into the trees, obliterating servo-motors left and right.

A posse of nervous military police arrested him when he and his crooked grin emerged on the far side.

He lost his sniper's badge and was sent to the stockade. While there he was posted to Vietnam but the army first foolishly gave him a week's leave. He spent it in Idaho with a band he used to play with. They all got drunk and he mentioned that he was not looking forward to his upcoming assignment and wished that he could avoid it. That is when somebody – either the drummer or the bass player, he never could remember – shot him in the kneecap. Musicians have always gone out of their way to help fellow musicians.

He was court-martialled for that and sent back to the stockade as soon as he got out of the hospital. After a while he was ordered, without a guard, to hobble across the parade ground to the Provost Marshal's to get tried, convicted and sentenced to a year or so in jail, then be dishonourably discharged as unfit to shoot people on behalf of the State.

There was a bus stop at one corner of the parade ground. He decided to skip the court-martial and hop the 1330 bus to the nearest airport. As a wounded serviceman, he was treated royally on the jet to Seattle. As a deserter, he was treated royally by the anti-war underground.

We loved Jumbo. He was funny and honest, naturally peaceable and a spooky sweet guitarist. He had left home at sixteen, bored with high school, and made a living playing underage in nightclubs and – more legally – at state fairs, where he was paid by the Fender company to demonstrate its equipment.

Jane grew to love Jumbo too. She was a young, orphaned, wild, Nearly Licensed Nurse who had been deported from the U.S. when she was discovered working there in an illegal abortion clinic. I had met her while she was a waitress at Chappy's Fish and Chips. She gave me and a lot of others free meals until her boss went bankrupt and she lost her job.

Jane and a rotation of hippies and draft dodgers lived next door. Those guys were always trying to get into her pants. The dodgers were the most insistent since she was unmarried. Marrying a Canuck was a shortcut to citizenship and the right to vote for every conceivable gradation of Canadian political candidate, nearly all socialist.

Suitors fawned over Jane. They bought beer. They shoplifted fine wines for her. They offered rare narcotics and bonbons. When these gifts did not always get them into her bedroom, they would throw themselves at her door. We could hear them at our house. She began coming over to our place whenever she needed to sleep.

Jumbo, despite his outlaw lip – or maybe because of it – was truly shy when he wasn't playing guitar. Jane was attracted to shy. Jumbo told her he didn't like nurses, and that Canadian women were boring. I guess he'd never met any of the girls from Kitchener-Waterloo where she had grown up. Beryl was her Matron of Honour and I was Best Man at their wedding.

By then our new foursome had moved into the Fraser Valley where we shared a haunted farmhouse with the Pork Belly Blues Band and an unattached redheaded drummer named Kelly, whose career as a symphony percussionist had come to an abrupt end when he fired off the cannons of the 1812 Overture three bars too soon.

The change was necessary: Michael and Julie were tiring of the wieners and beans Beryl and I could bring to the table; I was ashamed when they kept cooking up steak and lobster. Besides, Julie was pregnant. The Brewsters needed their home back.

Jumbo and Kelly and I put our last dimes into down payments on instruments and sound equipment, calling the resultant state of destitution the Justin band. Pork Belly and its entourage were committed "blues artists," which meant they didn't have any gear at all and always waited until we went to bed so they could jam with ours.

The house had two ghosts.

One was an old codger who had accidentally killed himself in 1923 when he slipped off a stool while changing an Edison electric light bulb. He liked to materialize just long enough for us to see him unscrewing the overhead light bulbs in the kitchen. It was a strange fetish but then I don't think the guy was "all there," if you know what I mean. Beryl tried to help him "find the light." I tried to talk him into actually changing bulbs for us instead of removing them and smashing them on the floor all the time. Neither of us was successful; the poor man was pretty well stuck in a rut.

Nobody ever saw the second ghost but all agreed that it was a baby hanging out between two of the upstairs bedrooms. Sometimes it would coo and gurgle, but it always cried after dark. With the baby crying and Pork Belly cranking on our equipment all night we often had a hard time going to sleep. Pork Belly mostly slept all day, so they got the baby's gurgles; we got the tears. It wasn't fair. Beryl could sometimes sing it to sleep but the sad little tyke persisted until Jane and Jumbo took a chainsaw to the wall dividing the bedrooms. The baby didn't cry after that. It didn't coo, either. Can a chainsaw be a tool of spiritual release?

Each of us had to raise seven dollars a month for rent. The women were the only ones who ever paid on time; they had found part-time work in the nearby town of Mission.

Because I wore glasses and at 23 was by far the oldest, I was elected to be our business manager; Jumbo was musical director. Managing an under-capitalized and unknown rock 'n roll band requires imaginative flare and a full knowledge of the business. I possessed neither, and will admit in retrospect that I made a few small blunders with Justin. Apologies are in order.

I apologize for not knowing that the studio I used to produce our demo tape would want actual cash before releasing the tape to us. At least we were never sued for the cost of our studio time.

I am sorry, Jumbo, for the confusion attending our first live performance. How was I to know that the junior high gym was in the same complex as the senior high gym where we were booked to do a Halloween dance? It was gonzo fate that both classes were throwing dances the same night and that I directed us to the wrong gym. Could've happened to anyone, but I will take responsibility. Remember how excited the junior high kids were to see us; the way they helped us carry in our equipment and set it up; the short skinny girl who asked for your autograph on her forehead; the way we joked that these people must be the most physically stunted community of 17-year olds in North America?

Were we surprised to learn of my mistake at the end of the night!

Thanks to my public relations ability we weren't sued by the senior high for breach of contract, and the junior high gave us four monstrous pumpkins. Fortunately Beryl made great pumpkin pie since that was all we had to eat for a week afterwards.

As a community service and to give us more public exposure I had us do a free show for the residents of Vancouver's Institute for the Deaf. Kelly was the star when the teachers let some of the smaller students crawl inside his bass drum and feel the concussions. I've always been sorry I didn't know their language and couldn't tell what they were signing with their fingers when we were through.

Just when it seemed that we were getting nowhere, Oz and Marybeth showed up from Missoula for a visit.

With a Master's degree in Performing Arts under her belt, Marybeth had become a Playboy bunny at one of Hugh Hefner's clubs in Panama. Except for having to wear velveteen rabbit ears four hours a day, she enjoyed the job and the country until a rising young army colonel named Noriega got the hots for her. She had rebuffed his advances because she thought he was a creep. For her own protection – and his – the club manager flew her back to the States where she was currently between jobs.

Oz was already the major shareholder and driving force behind the Lolo Building, a sort of counter-culture shopping mall in Missoula.

Their first night at the farm was spent catching up on the local gossip: who was in jail; who was dead; who had gone crazy; who was still on the loose. I politely waited until the next morning to hit him up for a six hundred buck loan. He forked it right over. I respect Oz, but the way he lets others take advantage of him has always made me uneasy. He and Marybeth could only stay for a couple of days before jetting to Mombasa to pick up some African trade items, but we all had a wonderful time together.

Jumbo and I used Oz's bankroll to finance a project that was certain to get Justin off the ground. We would rent the big hall that used to stand off Hastings Street near Exhibition Stadium in Vancouver. We'd buy air time on all the radio stations in the lower mainland. We'd plaster the city with posters and fill the newspapers with ads for our own rock concert: no agents or promoters; we could do the legwork ourselves. Jumbo said that this approach had worked well for him and his band in Idaho, and hadn't cost much either.

It may have been cheap in Idaho, but after renting the hall we only had enough left to buy a ten-second radio spot and get a few lines into the Classifieds of the *Sun*, where it was placed alongside a list of the city's upcoming bingo games.

We talked Pork Belly into making posters by hand in return for letting them be our warm-up act and getting 25% of the gate receipts. They went right to work, making almost twenty posters and tacking them to unfrequented telephone poles in Port Coquitlam, a charming industrial suburb at the far end of Vancouver Harbour. The posters read: the INCREDIBLE PORK BELLY BLUES BAND, with Justin, and more.

I suspect that concert would have been more successful if Justin instead of Pork Belly had been headlined on the posters. Who can honestly say? Our attendance was hurt more by the fact that a pretty popular English band called Led Zeppelin, along with Eric Clapton, was appearing that night at Exhibition Stadium. I had neglected to check with the other big promoters to find out what *they* were doing. Promoters can ruin each other through such oversights. Zeppelin and Clapton lost fourteen paying customers to us; we lost 15,833 to them.

I don't think Oz was ever repaid for his loan. I should do that real soon.

The Enforcers

With the future looking mighty bleak and the present drizzling on our heads, Dame Fortune – God bless her hot little hands – swept in to our rescue.

Jumbo and Kelly were invited to replace the drummer and guitarist in a local band called The Ace Tones (we invariably referred to them as the "acetones," in honour of that famous variant of the ketone chemical family). A carpet installer named Ted was the bandleader; his wife Connie was the singer.

The previous guitarist and drummer had been forced into early retirement as the result of a barroom altercation in which their wrists and knees had been broken by a mob of outraged patrons because they had both laughed when Connie fell off the stage and knocked herself out. It seems that Connie, who was a rotten singer, pretended to faint whenever she forgot the lyrics to a song she was butchering, or got caught expelling a particularly awful stream of sour notes. Over the years her audiences had convinced themselves that she must be gamely fighting a battle with throat cancer. They loved her. She usually contrived to collapse gracefully and harmlessly – legs together – at the base of her microphone stand, but this night she had drunk more than usual, overbalanced and taken the fall.

Her sidemen saw poetic justice, and guffawed; her fans saw red.

Ted laughed too. Because he was Connie's husband, the crowd only cracked a couple of his ribs before letting him run away. His sidemen weren't as lucky.

Do not think, however, that my friends abandoned me. They lied to a prison guard who was forming another weekend band; they told him that I was one of the best guitar players in the west.

Despite his fantasized machismo, zodiac necklace and self-admitted rudimentary drumming skills, curly-headed Dale James gave me a better education in how to be a successful bar musician than anyone I ever met. What is more, he was generous and kind-hearted. He took an unlikely pack of misfits and turned us into the most popular four-piece in the Fraser Valley, more in demand than the Ace Tones. We were called The Enforcers.

Dale, if you're reading this, I want to thank you here and now. I should also explain how it came about that your wife and I decided to take the kids and leave you...

...There are thousands of weekend bands in North America, and they play a vital role in their communities. They are a sort of shallow pond in which tadpole musicians get their start, and to which the burnt-out, cirrhosis-ridden, toad-like husks that were road musicians return after years in the swamp. They perform at all the local weddings, service clubs and smaller bars for less money than a traveling road band could charge. The money spent to hire a weekend band stays right in the area. As a matter of fact, much of it is spent right at the point of earnings on beer and marijuana and junk food.

Dale was our front man, boss of the show when we were on stage. Except for me, everyone in the band had a real job with the British Columbia Corrections Service.

Trish was an unmarried secretary with lungs like bellows, a tender heart and a weight problem. RCA Victor had offered her a recording contract, with the proviso that she had to lose 40 pounds or grow six inches. She tried her best, but was still 37 pounds and six inches on the dark side of true fame. Welcome to the country music industry.

She was a romantic girl, breaking into tears whenever she sang *Cry Me a River.* Dale had her sing it twice a night.

Sammy was one of the province's best parole officers and worst bassists. There were no such things as time signatures, tempos or keys in Sammy's world. What he had in spades was ebullience and the attention span of a small child, traits that endeared him to country folks.

We practiced in Dale's garage, which he had converted into a studio. It also served as a bachelor's pad for his own use on the nights when Denise threw him out of their house.

Raven-haired Denise was his wife and mother of their young family. She had encouraged her husband's artistic side when he first came out of the closet with his drum kit, but grew to dislike us all as more and more gigs came our way. It was nothing personal: Dale was in the garage practicing with us nearly every night we weren't out of town playing at some club. Being from Cape Breton, where women wear their hearts on their sleeves and behave like women are supposed to, she started banishing the poor guy to the studio on the rare occasions they were alone together.

"I won't be your afterthought," she told him.

We all felt sympathy for Dale; although he loved to flirt from the stage, he was – to my mind – ridiculously faithful to at least the *idea* of having a wife and family. What more can one expect of a bar musician?

Beryl, who was left alone just as much, worked and watched.

Months passed. I practiced like a fiend, encouraging everyone else to do the same, so we could become a full-fledged road band. As if she wasn't good enough already, Trish had a string of tawdry affairs that left her singing like a diva. Sammy got into and out of major trouble with *his* wife and the government for turning his home into a halfway house for female parolees. The women were always attractive and invariably re-entered general society singing his praises. They had never heard him play bass.

Thanks to Dale's business acumen, Trish's voice and Sammy's charisma, we got hired to play premier events like the annual Hatzic Lake Elks Club Corn Roast. Though he was our leader, Dale always split our pay equally, so I made thirty and sometimes fifty dollars a week before expenses. With that and Beryl's clerking pay, the two of us rented a small place across the lane from the haunted house. Jumbo, Jane and Kelly moved out soon afterward, which forced Pork Belly – complaining bitterly about heartless governments – to slouch back into Vancouver in order to continue living solely on their welfare cheques.

It was nice to be alone together again.

I have never completely understood why Beryl married me. She had (still has) a delightfully aberrant personality, but that is hardly reason enough. I know she was having trouble reconciling her ideal of me the impoverished political exile with me the impoverished and unpromising musician. True, I was still wanted by the FBI for draft evasion, counseling draft evasion, fomenting riots, suspicion of destruction of military property, and leaving the U.S. without permission; now I was also wanted by the General Motors Acceptance Corporation for being in arrears on our van payments. How the great had fallen. I think that if I had maintained my ties with the American political underground, written polemics or appeared to be suffering even a little bit for sticking to my beliefs, she would have supported me forever; but I was obviously having a wonderful time. She decided to assert herself, and asked that I start washing the dishes every other day.

I don't know about you, but I personally hate the notion of *having* dishes, much less washing them. Think about it for a minute. If you have dishes you still need pots and pans because dishes are purposely made to melt or explode in the oven or over open flames. If you have dishes you will want bowls because dishes are made too flat to hold much soup. If you have bowls you will want cups and mugs, because the bowls don't have handles to allow you to pick them up when they're hot. If you have either bowls or cups you will want saucers; I don't know why, but you will. Then you'll require special cupboards in which to store all this, so it won't get dusty until you want to get it dirty again. It goes without saying that you'll want a tablecloth or two for them to sit on while you take the hot food out of the pots and pans and put it on the dishes to get cold for a while before you eat it. A tablecloth calls for a table, and that calls for chairs because most of our tables are too low to be of use to a person who is standing up and too low to be of use to a person sitting on the floor. We have all been duped by a cabal of ceramic con artists and cabinet makers into thinking this stuff is worthwhile. Consider all the money wasted on tables and chairs and dishes that could be used to buy sound equipment, for instance. Imagine how our quality of life could be improved if we all spent an extra half-hour a day making music or making love instead of washing dishes.

Holding firmly to my principles, I refused her request. She actually raised her voice and accused me of taking a free ride at her expense. By her lights, she was right, of course. When I couldn't convince her to let me chuck out our spare bowl and extra fork and make love instead, it became necessary for me to leave and be a burden to her no longer.

I spent a miserable night trying to sleep in the drainage ditch in front of Dale and Denise's driveway. Dale saw me there in the morning as he left to guard some more prisoners. He generously offered to let me move into the studio.

Beryl and I were still on talking terms; I even spent a couple of days building her a rickety fence to keep the deer and the neighbours' plow horse out of the garden that had become her new joy. She invited me to stay for supper, without having to wash the dishes.

"How are things down the road, lover?" she asked.

"Mmm, really good," I replied through a mouthful of corn on the cob.

"And how is Denise?"

"Denise? I don't know. Don't see much of her."

"You will," she said with a twinkle in her eye. By the way, I made some curtains for you. And you can have the coffeepot. Take them when you have to go."

I'll be darned if Beryl wasn't right about Denise.

Denise began inviting me over for coffee and homemade cookies while Dale was at work. We had long conversations about the things that mattered to her: her two young children, her home, her marriage. She was the first "straight," outwardly normal woman I had met since leaving suburbia in 1964. I felt honoured by her confiding manner and the electrical ways our knees touched under the kitchen table. *I take it all back; there is a use for kitchen tables.*

Other visits followed, always while Dale was gone. If Denise wasn't baking cookies she was baking cakes or pies. She sure baked a lot. As we got to know each other better I was more and more impressed with her practical intelligence and the way she held my hands in hers while speaking of Dale and her fears that she was losing him to the band.

"He always used to be home at night. I liked that," she said. "Then the children were born and things changed. He started playing in these damned bands. Excuse me, I know you're part of one, but that's how I feel about them. I don't think he loves me anymore." Tears welled in her soft brown eyes. I hugged her like a brother. Sort of.

"Denise, he still loves you." God, her breasts felt warm, even through the sweater and brassiere.

"He doesn't act like it."

"Then he is a jerk," I said. "You're a fine person. And, if you don't mind my saying so, you're gorgeous too." I let go of her before I did something foolish. As it was, I collapsed in a breathless sweat on the wall-to-wall carpet. Women affect me that way.

"Do you really think I'm pretty?" the poor girl seemed pleased.

"Just look at yourself." We both scrutinized her body from our different perspectives.

"You don't think I'm too fat?" she was teasing now, not seeking reassurance.

"Here's what *I* think," I said, gently drawing her hands toward my pants.

That is when the baby woke from his nap and started to cry, which woke the toddler from *her* nap. Motherhood called and Denise excused herself. I walked stiffly across the yard to the studio.

Day followed day with the inevitability of a meteor plunging to earth. More gigs for more money from Dale. More smiles from Beryl. More cookies and confidences from Denise: Dale was sexually ignoring her, taking her for granted, threatening to take the band on a road tour. More and better adolescent fondling and kissing. I was in a state of constant sensual delirium that was only heightened by the way her children would wake up crying from their naps. I didn't always hear them, but Denise could. She said that Cape Breton women grew up being able to hear the fish breathe. Anyway, her cute little croakers will never know the number of times they brought their mother back from the verge of adultery; down from the skies of gratuitous sex to the mown lawn of regular family life. Two, three times maybe? I can't remember. I always lose track after one.

"How is Denise?" asked Beryl, treating me to another meal. The summer smell of sweetwater poplar was all around us.

"Not so well, love. She and Dale are having hard times."

"Kind of like us, huh?" she smiled that irresistible psychic smile.

"Are you having a hard time? I mean, your garden looks great...the breeze is warm...you know I still love you."

"Do I?"

One afternoon Denise cried and said that she had finally decided to take the kids and leave Dale. She was going to talk to him in the evening. I think I was influential in encouraging her to assert herself this way, and reminded her that sometimes people had to leave each other before they could get back together. I suggested that, meanwhile, she and I and the children could rent a house somewhere. She nodded agreement. She didn't feel like petting, but kissed me goodbye. It wasn't even a French kiss, so I knew she was distracted.

Back in the studio, I saw Dale come home. I wondered how Denise was doing. I wondered how Dale was taking the news. I wondered how I was going to explain to him why I was moving in with his wife. I wondered how I was going to get the money to rent a real house and feed a real family. I wondered how Beryl was going to take the changed state of affairs without feeling jilted. Oh well, *Be yourself and turmoil will follow naturally* was my motto. I fell asleep wondering.

Dale slammed his way into the studio at dawn. I was ready with a pot of fresh coffee. I make coffee for these occasions. The custom started in college; Barb Palin (no relation to the future Alaska governor) and I were in bed together when her husband and the city bailiff barged into 809 East Front to serve her with her divorce papers. With our passion at a temporary ebb and the bailiff ill-at-ease, I got up and made us all coffee. It seemed like a friendly thing to do.

"Good morning Dale. Want some?" I lifted the pot for him to see.

"You know where you can put your coffee."

"What's the matter?" I can't believe I really said that, but I did. You have to get to the point somehow.

"Denise has told me all about you. You're like Charles Manson. You're very sick."

"Charles Manson, the ritual murderer?"

"Yeah. The one who hypnotized and drugged women to kill for him. You tried to use Denise to kill our marriage."

"I *what*?"

"Only it didn't work. Denise didn't break after all. I should beat the hell out of you, you sunuvabitch." Dale was shaking with anger.

"Listen, Denise said that lately you and she..."

He cut me off. "Shut up. Why did you give her the LSD?" He started to weep. "Gary, if you hadn't been my friend you'd be in jail right now for what you tried to do to her. You didn't even tell her, did you? Just slipped it into her... coffee... or something, eh?"

I didn't have a clue what he was talking about.

"Be honest for once in your sick life," he continued. "Why did you do it? Are you jealous of me? The things I have, like Denise? Is that it? Never mind. It's all okay now. She's in bad shape, but she'll be alright in time."

I was beginning to get the impression that Denise had not told Dale quite what she told me she was going to tell Dale. Those cookies. Those hands in my pants. What a woman. What a mind!

"I guess that means I'm fired," I said.

"No, you're not fired," said Dale. "Nobody is fired. Just get out. And don't come back. Take the band with you. I quit. After what you've done, Denise is going to need a lot of help to recover. I'll be there. Thank Christ I wasn't too late." In an agony of guilt, he broke down. We sat there in the studio for some time.

I could have argued with Dale, but anyone who believed I would feed his wife lysergic acid in order to steal his family is probably past the stage of reasonable discussion. Besides, I can enjoy a good joke, and like to see a fitting resolution to a contest of wills. Dale and I had both been tooled by a Cape Bretoner. Looking on the bright side, I wouldn't need to find a way to support an entire family after all. Denise believed in dishes much more than Beryl did; Dale would wash them now. I felt that he was renouncing magic for marriage, but many people do that. Not everyone is meant to be a bar musician.

How could I best help this man? By paying Denise one final compliment.

"I am sorry for all this," I said softly. "I'm leaving now. I am going to get some psychiatric help. My mind is a mess these days. But I want you to know from someone who was once your friend, I only gave your wife a few micrograms of LSD when she wasn't looking; and she is the hardest person to hypnotize that I have ever met."

Home Sweet Home

Canceling our gigs.

Sleeping on Sammy's couch.

Stopping Sammy from going over to Dale's "to beat some sense into his head."

Saying goodbye to Trish as she leaves on the Greyhound to go to hairdressing school.

Promising myself to always remember that women are incredibly smart.

Walking through miles of August to see Beryl.

She is in the garden, teary-eyed and trying to laugh.

There is no garden fence left standing.

There is no lettuce.

No tomatoes.

No onions.

No carrots.

No squash or pumpkins.

The neighbours' plow horse is chomping her last bunch of radishes and daring her to do something about it.

"He just leaned on it and it fell over," she says. "Whoompf! I tried to keep him out, but every time I turned my back he'd come in and eat more. I really liked the pumpkins. I guess he did, too."

"I'm so sorry, lover. Wasn't much of a fence, was it?"

"No. It was the worst fence I have ever seen, but it wasn't much of a garden anyhow," she says.

"It was a beautiful garden."

"I'm not a good gardener, but I tried to make it grow."

"I thought it was wonderful. So did the horse."

"Do you want to stay for supper?" she asks.

"I would like that. And you can call me Charles Manson."

"It's only cornbread, Chuck. There was supposed to be salad, too."

"Who needs salad when he's having supper with you?"

In a Pinch, You Can Always Kill Yourself

Word got out around the valley that you couldn't trust me with your wife, so it is understandable that nobody wanted me to play in their band. When Beryl's hours at the department store were cut, we moved to a dirt-cheap cabin up by Stave Lake. We were consistently hungry by November and downright skinny by January when she left to look for full-time work in Vancouver. I stayed behind because I had finally got a job splitting cedar shakes for a local outfit. I lived on nothing but potatoes for an entire month, waiting for a paycheque that bounced higher than a rubber ball shortly after it arrived.

Evicted from the cabin, I joined Beryl in the city. She had been living solely on rice herself, but had landed a job with Social Services. She was staying in a rundown motel while she saved money to get green vegetables and an apartment. She took me in, which was darned decent of her when you consider the circumstances.

Her birthday was in March, and when it came I had 20¢ left to my name. I bought her a day-old cupcake; it broke my heart when she thanked me and offered to split it between us.

Nadir.

I kissed her and said I was going for a walk.

I headed for Stanley Park to jump off the Lions Gate Bridge and be done with this sadness and humiliation.

Walking down Georgia Street for the last time, the traffic lights and store signs seemed brighter than ever; the smell of barbeque from the Texan Burger stand more piquant. Part of me was going to miss this place. The boats at the yacht club in Coal Harbour floated shimmering in the city lights. It was ebb tide and Brockton Point was alive with muskrats, otters and lovers making out in parked cars. Looming above the mist of a spring evening, Lions Gate was magnificent. By the time I reached it, I realized that I wasn't going to kill myself right away, so I listened to the hum of cars crossing high above the harbour mouth before going back to the motel where I curled up in a corner of the room and cried.

Beryl had been worried about me – she was a glutton for punishment. She called friends in Kamloops who sent money to buy me a bus ticket out of town. I could stay at their house while I looked for work. They were both former Americans who had immigrated north at the same time we had.

They fattened me up and let me stay until I found a job in Ashcroft, a village in a sagebrush canyon along the Thompson River. I worked there for half a year as a janitor-orderly, keeping things clean and even helping to extend one patient's life when I stopped a nurse from administering nitrogen instead of oxygen.

I bunked in the Ashcroft Hotel, where my dad and his new girlfriend, Ruth, came to visit. They seemed very happy together. I splurged and rented them a room with a king-sized bed, which they politely declined because they weren't yet married. Ruth was a born-again Christian, and fussy about Biblical transgressions. I guess I didn't look as prosperous as I felt, because they bought me a fan to cool my room, which was stiflingly hot in the summer.

Some Friday nights I would hitchhike to the outdoor drive-in theatre at Cache Creek, pay my two bucks to go sit in a parking stall with the car speaker on my lap, and watch a movie. I have Beryl and her friends to thank for getting me there, propped against the speaker post, keeping an eye cocked for rattlesnakes, feeling mighty upscale and full of self-worth.

Other weekends I'd hitch to Vancouver to be with Beryl. She, too, was eating regularly again. We'd spend hours in Stanley Park.

Ever since the car wreck, my back has had its own way of telling me that it's time to change jobs, so when I began cramping and falling over in the halls of Ashcroft Hospital I moved back to the coast. Beryl and I rented a place we called Willingdon House.

Jumbo and Jane also moved in, along with Charlie Pontefract, who had been in South America buying pre-Colombian artifacts for resale. A tribe had gathered, and Willingdon was its longhouse.

Jumbo and I formed a commercial bar band called Skyhook, found it an agent, put it aboard a freighter steaming up the coast to a fishing port near Bella Coola, and played some good music for good money. The Quixicum First Nation had finished making its old village uninhabitable and had just built and moved to a new town on an island a mile offshore. The natives were our primary audience, mixed with a few Anglo fishermen who sat on barstools talking to themselves; and I don't mean talking *among* themselves, I mean talking *to* themselves. Lost at sea.

The folks of Quixicum were friendly and sociable hosts, ferrying us over for visits to New Town, as they called it. We often had dinner at the chief's house. I developed a fondness for oolichan oil, which is the slick soup you get by stuffing small bony fish into a rusty oil drum to rot for a month, very similar to the way you make wine – only you don't have to stomp in it barefooted.

The toughest part of the chief's job lay in trying to keep everyone sober, for one of his nieces was paying her way through law school by chartering helicopter deliveries of booze every few days from the government liquor store in Bella Coola. The whole population would troop over to the helipad and buy cases off the tarmac at fifty dollars a bottle. Families would go home, get drunk and knife each other with wild abandon. The chopper pilot always stuck around for a few hours, making some extra money flying the injured to the Bella Coola hospital on his return trip.

Skyhook was a "happening" band for months, which was a lifetime as bands went in those days. Many of our gigs were in the city, so Jumbo and I got to be home a lot, enjoying the sun as it shone down on Willingdon.

The weather wasn't as fine for our drummer, who was having marital problems. One day he walked into the office tower where his wife worked, yanked up her skirt and ripped off her panties in front of the astonished staff, stuck them between his teeth and rode up and down on the elevators until the police came and bundled him away to the funny farm. Drummers are not like you and me.

We broke in a new guy by booking some jobs at grubby strip clubs on Hastings Street. One was at an upstairs dive called Bubba's. We played and strippers stripped to an eerily empty room all week. Not one customer entered the premises until Saturday night when the bouncer padlocked the entrance to keep out the riff raff while a heavyset man with a pockmarked face appeared from nowhere and commandeered the front table.

"Play good," he said.

Since there was a reasonable chance that we were looking at our boss, we played very well indeed. I don't know how much he liked the music; don't know how much he liked the free drinks or the girls who took off all their clothes and danced for him; he sat there stone-faced for a set before disappearing into the gloom at the back where the toilets were. We never saw him again.

The bouncer unlocked the entrance. No one else walked in all night. The bartender handed us our week's pay without comment. We decided to add another guitar player.

Charlie was available.

He was in a bit of trouble with the Better Business Bureau for trying to sell the University of BC fake pre-Colombian pottery. It wasn't his fault; he had paid top dollar for reputedly real stuff to a Bogota art dealer who had been recommended to him by an acquaintance he had met in a San Diego bar after delivering a ketch down there for a businessman from Victoria who didn't have the time to make the passage himself.

Charlie had been forced to foist onto local art dealers a certain amount of misrepresented gold-coloured jewellery and leaky clay pots. He felt bad about having to do that, but said legitimate collectors should know what they're doing. Adding insult to injury, he had been run off the streets by those same art dealers for trying to make an honest buck by discounting his remaining pieces outside their storefronts for less than they had paid.

"What happened to free enterprise? This sure as hell ain't America," he complained.

Charlie was a quick study. Before you could say "sex, drugs, and rock 'n roll," we were off to play in Prince Rupert, a gazillion miles north by highway.

We were fired on opening night, minutes after the ambulances left the club. Some unattached brain cells in Charlie's cerebral cortex had told him that it would be flashy to end one of our songs by leaping off the stage and sliding on his knees across the jam-packed dance floor. He cut quite a swath through the crowd, men went down as if they'd been chop-blocked, women flew through the air like bowling pins. Only a few had to be hospitalized. You always knew when Charlie was in town.

That was the end of Skyhook. Jumbo threw in the towel and enrolled in welding school; Charlie headed for the Caribbean to join the crew of Bitterroot Al's banana boat. I looked around for another band.

One Penny Opera

Barbara grows up tall and beak-nosed in Montreal. She has an incredible vocal range and an emotional palette to match it. Her favorite songwriter is Wolfgang Mozart. She is a vegetarian with a part-time voice coach and a boyfriend named Stuart, who plays decent jazz guitar. He looks like her, but with a black Fu Manchu moustache.

Neither has ever played in a bar.

No problem. Besides, we've formed a band, need an equipment van, and Barbara owns one.

I supply the sound system, the bass and a booking agent who in turn finds a closet drummer whose parents want him to leave home. After a couple of weeks of rehearsal we pile into the van and head north 500 miles to the mill city of Prince George for our maiden gig.

The *Greenchain Club* has a booming interior the size of a school gymnasium, with an ambiance to match. The stage is unusually high – about four feet above one end of the dance floor. It is protected with light-gauge chicken wire. During sound check, Barbara complains to me that the mesh will separate and isolate her from her audience.

"That could be the reason for it, alright," I say.

"They must have had some pretty bad acts in here," she says.

We play our first set to a smattering of applause as the club fills up with mill workers and off-shift waitresses. Barbara's 45 minutes of unforgettably loud operatic warm-ups in the parking lot seem to be paying dividends. She does a good job on some rhythm and blues standards. The miniskirt and long legs draw attention away from the Duke of Wellington nose.

The patrons' interest in our music increases during the second set. Guys grab tables close to the stage. Some wander singly onto the dance floor in front of us, looking up Barbara's skirt before going to the urinals; taking a closer look on the way back to their tables. Some people may think such behavior to be demeaning or obscene. I don't. I maintain that it is honest human interaction fostered and shaped by the rich tonalities of live musical performance.

I notice a few small, wiry men in turbans coming into the club. They stand by themselves in a corner. I remember reading in the newspapers about the "minor influx" of Sikhs into the BC interior...disputes over whether or not they can be fired for not wearing hardhats on industrial jobsites if their religion forbids them to remove their turbans in public...Can a hardhat be worn over a turban?... Can a turban be wrapped religiously around a hardhat?...What happens to the wearer if a turban becomes unwrapped and catches in the greenchain?...What is our reference point here, the Koran or BC Industrial Safety Regulation 72/040?

Meanwhile Barbara is not completely at ease with all the men staring up her legs. She urges them to pay more attention to her voice than her body by improvising on the melody and lyrics of a rock classic.

"Just sing the fucking words!" somebody shouts to general agreement. The set ends. Barbara hurries out of the room to change into a pants suit.

Back onstage we find our groove. Stuart has smoked a joint and had a beer during the break. He plays monster guitar over, under, around and through the solid beat the drummer and I construct for him. Barbara gets down to business and belts out the songs with power and only an occasional flight of soprano fancy. The dance floor is near to springing its joists with loggers and sawyers and waitresses and wives and truckers and hookers. It is turning into a hot night in Prince George. Then one of the Sikhs mistakes a foreman's daughter for a potential dance partner and gets punched in the nose. The club manager appears from nowhere to see what the fuss is about; watches as the poor man with the bloody face and the turban stumbles around the dance floor. A second turban steps away from the far wall and joins him. They look like they are dancing together. We are playing a slow, emotive, pelvis-grinding ballad made for lovers. The Sikhs feel the music. They wrap their arms around one another...Barbara sees them, and is moved...*Oh yeah, can ya feel it?* she croons.

The men of Prince George are not homophobic: women can dance in complete safety with other women at any bar in town, as long as they don't act butch. But there *are* unwritten rules of conduct for bar patrons throughout the North, and at the *Greenchain* they are also hand printed in rustproof black spray paint on the front of the building:

NO HIPPIES

SHIRTS AND SHOOZ MUST BE WORN AT ALL TIMES

NO QUEERS

SIX PAXS TO GO...

Plaid flannel shirts and red suspenders fold over the dancing men like pond lilies or maybe skunk cabbage leaves at sundown. When they move apart a minute later, there is no trace of the Sikhs. I believe they have been eaten. Seeing that everything is back to normal, the manager relaxes.

"That was horrible. Those poor men," says Barbara on our next break. "They really like me, though! This is fun! I'm looking forward to tomorrow already!"

She says good night.

"We still have two hours to play," I tell her.

"Not me," she says, her face turning to stone. "My vocal coach would dismiss me. Sing five hours a night, plus warm-ups? That's ridiculous!"

"That's the contract."

"*I* didn't sign it."

She has a good point. *I* signed it. It is a standard club performance contract, and calls for a five-hour show six nights a week, plus a two-hour matinee or jam session on Saturday afternoon. It is so standard that I haven't mentioned any details to the band except our $800 a week fee, less 15% agent's commission.

"But you're our singer," I say weakly.

"And I will not ruin my voice for you or these people," she replies on her way out the door.

I find Stuart and the drummer toking up in the parking lot; ask them if they can do our vocals for a couple of hours. The drummer shakes his head. Stuart says he will try; that he knows the words to some blues tunes.

What he hasn't said, but what soon becomes obvious to everyone as we kick into the fourth set, is that he only remembers a few words of any given song. Also, he mutters rather than sings what few lyrics he does recall. Also, he can't play guitar and mutter at the same time.

The crowd starts zinging beer bottles.

The chicken wire screens us pretty well at first, although we get splattered with a lot of beer. The manager returns to see what the ruckus is about. He counts the bodies on stage, puckers his lips, folds his arms, stares up into the gypsum-lined ceiling. I guess he is waiting for something else to happen.

I am right. He is waiting for his clientele to recall from deep within their shared genetic memory that if they pitch their bottles over the wire instead of at it the arcs of brown glass which are thereby traced will land on the drummer's head. It doesn't take long for everyone to remember this, and a minute more before our one-man percussion section cowers cut, bleeding and beer-sticky beneath his snare drum and a crash cymbal.

The manager shrugs his shoulders, dims the stage lights, yanks the power cords to our equipment, hollers that we're fired, and buys a round for the house.

Children of the Sixties

Julie Brewster and her baby son moved into Willingdon House after she broke up with Michael. She and I were seriously in lust with each other. Since I was also very much in lust with Beryl, things could have been tricky – but they weren't. After all, we were the Children of the Sixties.

We became a band, and a fairly successful one at that. For more than two years we performed at small clubs and Legion halls around the province. Let's face it: sex sells, and people piled through the doors to see two beautiful women who could also sing. I am certain that nobody came to see or hear me, but I was happy.

One of our contracts was at a fancy strip club (yes, there is such a thing) on Granville Street. The province was in the hands of the New Democratic Party, which was union-oriented, and the NDP helped the musician's union by making it unlawful for anyone to remove all their clothes and dance naked in a public place unless they did so to the musical accompaniment of a live band or orchestra. Some musicians thought it was demeaning to back up strippers. We had no such high opinion of our talents, and the dancers we played for were mostly fine people who needed money to feed their children and their habits, just like you and me, only with an honest appreciation of the world around them. They came from all over: Asia, Ontario, the USA, Mozambique, even the Royal Winnipeg Ballet.

Strangely enough – and this says something about human nature – the single best striptease ever performed in that club was made by Charlie, returned from the tropics for a weekend. He brought down the house on amateur night; had jaded patrons jumping on the chairs, pounding on the tables and ordering doubles. He pantomimed the whole thing; never removed a stitch. He danced bashfully; he danced brazenly; he did a pratfall and then flopped across the stage like a breaching whale while pretending to erotically pull off his pants. He finished the show by giving lap dances to the audience, which fell over itself in hysterics and a rush to stuff money into his jeans and the pockets of his L.L. Bean down vest.

These were rich days. When we weren't booked out of town, life at Willingdon House became almost domestic – if you ignore the masturbating Jamaican we took in from off the street and whom I had to threaten with a tire iron to get to leave. We all changed the baby's diapers a lot and let him teach us how to smear food over our faces just like he did.

Beryl's family frequently crossed the border to visit, as did my brother and sister.

Fay had paid her own way through university; after his experience with me, Dad wouldn't help her. Sorry, Sis. She always came to town bringing hugs and kisses and a mule train of boyfriends; even immigrated here with one of them until hard times and an offer to teach English literature at an Idaho college took her back south to become a poet and liberal spirit in a state where a good home is one that possesses its own water supply and a clear field of fire.

Ken had long since dropped out of high school – he had been the student body president – after catching the football coach illegally transferring student body funds to the athletic department budget. He appealed the coach's actions to the faculty, much like I had done in Missoula. The faculty told him to shut up, so he led a boycott of classes that resulted in the return of the money and his own suspension; he was now a short order cook and weekend musician. We were more than brothers: it was as if we had the same part in a very quirky play. Comedy? Tragedy? Drama? Time would tell. I hoped that whoever wrote the script was a pro. Nobody wants to be stuck with bad lines.

The Cosmic Implications of Jumbo's Picket Fence

I think, therefore I am.
Rene Descartes

I think I think,
Therefore I think I am.
Ambrose Bierce

We visited Jumbo and Jane when the band played in Dawson Creek, whose claim to fame is being the start of the Alaska Highway. Jumbo had a job pressure-welding oil pipelines. He also had a story to tell.

Back in our Justin days he once mentioned a dream he'd had of being on stage, holding his guitar and laughing fit-to-bust. He was in some kind of band, but didn't know any of the four players up there with him.

"Do you remember me telling you about that?" he asked.

"Yes. And you said the stage had green astro turf with a white picket fence around it. That was sure a tacky dream," I added.

"God, you've got a mind for trivia. I'd forgotten all about it, and it was *my* dream. Anyhow, Jane and I had been here a month or so when we decided to drop in at the Mile Zero hotel for the weekly jam session. I brought my Stratocaster, had a couple of drinks and got up on stage with the house band. They weren't bad; we did the usual cover tunes; it was fun.

"Then the frontman decides to tell the crowd a joke. Some dumb joke, but it struck me as funny. I laughed out loud.

"Then it hit me. Here I was, on a stage with four guys I didn't know from Adam, and – spooky, spooky – the stage at the Zero is green astro turf surrounded by a white picket fence! My memory didn't kick in until I laughed, which is where the dream started. How weird is that!"

True story.

And I would bet big money that you and nearly everyone you know has a similar tale to tell.

I suggested to Jumbo that there were some logical deductions to be made here: there is no free will; it's pre-destination; our lives have already been lived; we are simply experiencing them moment by moment; Time is really an act of reveling in the details of the Great Tapestry; the fine skinny thread of our individual existence sometimes curls back across itself and we get *déjà vu* flashes like Jumbo's.

Does this mean most of us won't worry and "plan ahead" and stop thinking we have choices to make? Nope, because we have already done that – couldn't help ourselves. What it *does* mean is that the word *should* has no force and effect. I *shouldn't* do anything. I *will do* what I must, what I have already done but don't yet consciously know about. Individually we pray that we are one of the Tapestry's bright, strong and useful threads, not some mangy chunk of dog hair.

We all talked philosophy for a long time. It was clear that my friends thought I had taken one acid trip too many along the way, but we felt good being together again. We ended up going downtown to the Mile Zero to drink beer and look at the green rug with its white picket fence.

Head-banger and the Egg

The medicine show rages as black crow babies
peel love off the sidewalk, and the Family moves on...
Beryl Wright

And so it came to pass that we all loved as honestly as we could, and little by little found the threads of our lives separating in the Great Tapestry.

Even with help from Beryl and me, raising her son in the back seat of a '49 Plymouth and a series of cheap hotel rooms was not what Julie wanted. She met a great hulking, divorced Dutchman with a young family of his own, and Julie finally found a truly kindred spirit. They are still together.

Maybe it was the moon or high tides on Mars, all our stars and relationships were realigning: Jane and Jumbo split up; she fell in love with my brother-in-law, whose marriage to Beryl's sister Mae had fallen apart; Mae got together with my brother; my sister and mother raced each other to see who could be married the most times – got all that? Jumbo received a pardon from the U.S. government. He returned south to take over his dad's one-man TV gizmo business and turn it into a flourishing electronic components company. Even *my* name was in the last batch of presidential pardons signed by Jimmy Carter, though for some reason the FBI kept staking out my dad's place every time they tapped the phone and heard I might be coming back to visit.

Beryl got sick of popping birth control pills and decided to become a mother. Being a father is serious business, and I have always hated being serious for longer than is necessary. Who in the world would want me to be their parent? You could say that my sporadic non-compliance with the future as she saw it led her into the arms of others, but that wouldn't be true, for we were already often in the arms of others. These were the days when the #1 song in North America was a Crosby, Stills and Nash tune that said, "If you can't be with the one you love, love the one you're with." Regardless of whom their father might be, she promised to raise her daughters on her own; to be a burden to no one. This showed rare insight on her part, for there wasn't an ounce of father material in any of us men. And, yes, she said they would be daughters. She knew. And she was right – twice.

Oz and Charlie and I were with her when Lillian was born.

Charlie and I were with her when Ava was born.

For some inscrutable reason – we certainly weren't worried about breaking social conventions – she named me their dad.

Thank you, Beryl. A trio entered your lottery of love, but you settled on me when you had to fill in the blanks on the birth certificates. I am honoured.

Hi, Lil. I have loved you since the day you came into this world, looking like a blonde Balt. I must now tell everyone that I nicknamed you The Headbanger because of the way you always ran your head into the nearest wall to calm yourself for sleep. You might have permanent brain damage. Keep an eye out for symptoms, okay?

Hi, Ava. I have loved you since the day you came into this world, looking like a wizened Cherokee medicine woman. I must now tell everyone that I nicknamed you The Egg because of the way you always curled into a fetal position whenever anyone told you something you didn't want to hear. Now that you are grown up, if you are still doing that, perhaps you should stop.

Beryl was as good as her word, and raised the girls pretty much on her own. Over the years I have tried to help in typical ways, once by driving around town for a week with a claw hammer in the pickup to be used to break the kneecaps of a guy who had punched Ava while she was working a night shift. The Mounties got to him before I did.

My riskiest paternal action occurred the night after Beryl came home from the hospital with newly born Lil. Oz, Charlie and bunch of us were still celebrating her birth with way too much booze when a local guy we had met – and didn't particularly like – tried to crash the party. I told him to go away; he said he would come back and burn our house down. I thought about calling the police, but we were unknown newcomers to the village, so I grabbed my knife and stumbled drunkenly over to the guy's house to stab him in the guts. My friends would guard our place in the meantime.

I figured it was a good plan.

To his everlasting credit, Charlie sobered up quickly when he saw things were spiraling out of control. Rather than try to stop me, which would have been very difficult, he ducked down some alleys, got to the guy's house before I did and dragged him out the back door with a warning that I was on my way to kill him; that he ought to leave town for a few days while everybody simmered down. That's why nobody was there when I kicked in his door and sat down on the front steps to wait for him.

After an hour or so, Charlie "dropped by" and asked innocently if I'd seen the guy yet. When I said no, but it was my intention to eviscerate anyone who threatened my daughter, he agreed completely and gave me some speed to help me stay awake. Friends. He had pulled the old Grand Coulee Switcheroo and fed me Valium instead. I passed out; woke up in the morning at the foot of the steps and without a knife. Charlie gave it back in the fullness of time.

This all happened in a small mountain village called New Denver. The town was cobbled together by raiding American miners during a short-lived silver rush to the Kootenays a hundred years ago. Ten blocks long and a few blocks wide, it hangs either side of the stony Carpenter Creek delta on the shore of a long, glacier-fed lake called Slocan.

So far New Denver has not achieved the prominence of its American namesake, but it does boast of some nice clapboard houses, a traffic light and upwards of 600 residents, a third of whom are retirees who live the Canadian dream by spending most of each winter playing golf in Scottsdale, Arizona.

Depending on your point of view and what you ate for breakfast, the quaint little burg is a Shangri-la or a natural prison. You can get here from the north or east across scenic mountain passes, or from the south by driving up the Slocan River valley and negotiating a hanging wall known as the Slocan bluffs. The west is sealed by the lake and the Valhalla mountain range. In 1942 you could also get here by being a Japanese-Canadian citizen from the west coast, having all your assets seized and sold for a pittance, and being shipped inland by the thousands under armed guard to keep you from assisting Imperial Japan to invade British

Columbia. In the 1960s you could get here by being a young Doukhobor whose parents refused to let you learn English, attend public school, believe in secular government, or see anything unusual in burning down each other's houses for the sake of religious testimony. The province built a reform school just for you in the village. Beneath the bright ice of Denver glacier you would share the rocky alluvial fan with loggers and miners, American political dissidents, university professors, writers, painters and potters, several retired British paratroopers, pot growers, a scam artist and an elderly female Belgian chemist who was with the anti-fascist underground in WWII.

Beryl and I had first seen the valley while visiting some friends from Missoula days who were homesteading nearby. She fell in love with the place and declared that this is where she would raise her family. I followed her here from the Northwest Territories after finishing a six-month contract as the bass player with the house band at the Yellowknife Inn, where I started playing pedal steel guitar and banjo to add variety to its sound.

On her arrival as a very pregnant mother-to-be, she was told that men come to the valley to fall in love and women come to get strong. How right that was.

I hadn't even had time to unpack in the dilapidated house she had rented for us when a tall, stringy couple bearing fresh farm eggs and a toddler showed up at our door. Beryl had already told me about them. He was a U.S. army deserter, she was a Canadian prairie girl who had married him as a political favour, the little boy was a sign of their affection and memento of a summer spent learning to tan hides on an Okanagan Indian reserve.

"Hi! I'm Donna Jean, but everybody calls me DJ," said the woman. "And this is Jim and our son Tristan, and you are Gary – we are going to play together in a band – and these are eggs for you both!" she handed them over with a laugh.

DJ had a wide open face that beamed like a full moon bothered only slightly by an unruly corona of strawberry hair. The rubber farm boots and Big Mac overalls weren't to my taste, but I liked the way her breasts kept popping out from behind her wide suspenders.

That is how I met the future First Lady of New Denver and my son, and how Beryl met one of the best friends of her life. Of course that didn't happen right away; it took more years of inevitable circumstance.

First the girls had to be born, then we had to form a band called Loose Change (like DJ had foreseen). Along the way I toured a season with a new-age vaudeville troupe called the Valhallalujah Rangers, a great show that made some money for its manager while at night all the performers shared sleeping bags under a leaky tarp. Jim and I fulfilled our part of the valley's reputation by falling in love often and fairly indiscriminately; Beryl and DJ did likewise as they grew strong enough to ditch us both. The day came when Beryl said, "I'll always love you, but Honey it's time for you to leave."

Obeying the dictates of fate and a long-suffering woman I holed up in our garage for a while, then moved into a pup tent in the woods near Rosebery. Beryl came looking for me one day to say that Dad was on his way up for a visit. I was ashamed to be thirty years old, estranged from my family, broke and living in an orange toy tent, so I disappeared when he was due to arrive.

I was becoming pretty experienced at being broke and alone. This time I didn't need any friends to help me get back on my feet. I shuffled off to Calgary and shared a flophouse on skid row until I landed a job backing up a hard-drinking, talented, self-destructive country and western singer by the name of Johnny Wild. By the time I got tired of getting Johnny on stage for his shows I was eating well, had my own booking agent, a pickup truck with a homemade camper on the back and a few dollars in the bank. Beryl and I had stayed in touch, so I knew that she and DJ had been living and raising the kids together.

She said that things were changing; she'd fallen in love with a mechanic named Jack; they had scraped together enough money to buy an old false-front schoolhouse in Rosebery, and were going to turn it into a Mexican restaurant and motorcycle repair shop.

She also told me that DJ might be ready to join a traveling band.

Ooo la la!

The Message

It was a warm evening in late May of '79, the night before the band was leaving on its summer tour. The air outside the Wild Rose Cantina and Restaurant was thick with the smell of spring flowers, fried beans and mole sauce.

For no understandable reason I started getting breathless. I wanted to cry.

I walked across the gravel parking lot to the pickup, climbed into the camper and broke into tears. This was not normal; I am a shallow guy who wakes up each morning happy to lace his tennis shoes without help. Now my hands were shaking.

Paper and pen. I needed a paper and pen. I was losing myself to something powerful and beyond any personal control. Maybe those drugs from the 60s were finally making themselves felt. Found some paper. LSD was never like this, except for the need to trust your soul while you're being washed away. Grabbed a pen and wrote.

I am having trouble breathing, and I don't know if my heart is broken or full. I have loved you, all three.

Tears smudged then ruined the ink of the letters. What was happening here? I looked out the camper's window at the little frontier café. The lights were on inside. It was near closing time. Beryl would be cleaning the kitchen; Jack would be stirring a last pitcher of Margarita grandes for the diners at table four; Lil and Ava would be asleep upstairs.

I was ineffably sad but complete. Was this how salmon felt after spawning? As if it belonged to someone else, I watched my arm reach for a fresh piece of paper.

I am having trouble breathing, and I don't know if my heart is broken or full. I have loved you, all three.

The arm wrote this over and over until the page was filled with the words. I have never felt so blue, been so happy and so much in love all at the same time.

I was about to die. That much was certain...

...Content with my fate, I kept the knowing of it to myself when I said goodbye in the morning. A pair of beautiful girls and a wonderful woman would live happy years with Jack. He would always be there for them. Beryl, Lil, Ava, *I have loved you, all three.* I handed Beryl a sealed letter with the night's writing inside; told her she would know when to open it; gave everybody a hug, a last look, then off to Alberta and forever.

DJ rode with Dan and Chas – the group's bassist and drummer – in the equipment van while I tailed a few hundred yards behind. I was careful not to get ahead of them so they wouldn't have to see me get killed. I had a hunch that it would be a car wreck. That was most likely. My eyes embraced each oncoming semi and badly driven car, every mile of mountain highway with a view to eternity. I was being gifted with a warm and sunny last run. After a stop for gas, DJ hopped into the pickup. She or Dan would often change vehicles so that I wouldn't feel left out of the group, even though Chas always had cold beer in his. I told her I wanted to be alone awhile. She looked quizzically at me, but left with good grace. I liked her far too much to take her on a death ride. We crossed the Rockies going eastward through the Alberta foothills and into the short grass country. Maybe I would fall asleep at the wheel, like Idaho in '66; never know what hit me.

We were booked to play a week in Camrose and I was still alive when we got there. By Wednesday we were drawing a full house and were held over for a second week. Not being dead yet got me to thinking how much I wanted to invite DJ out to supper. Not the whole roadhouse gang – just her; someplace casually friendly rather than romantic; somewhere public that couldn't conceivably upset Dan or Chas, who also liked her a whole lot. That was fine with DJ, so we went to a Boston Pizza franchise that was new in town. She ordered several beers and a small something with goat cheese.

Dinner was pleasant. When the waiter brought the bill, she pulled money from a worn cloth wallet to pay for her share. I said no, this was my invitation; the beers and the goat were on me. Commonplace stuff, but DJ teared up.

Again she pushed some bills at me. I shook my head. She was crying. I asked her what was wrong.

"I'm sorry," she tried to smile. "Nobody has ever asked me out – and paid for all the food. This is...new."

"See," self-consciously, like a little girl, she showed me her wallet. It was a more intimate act than making love. "I brought money. You don't have to do this. No one else does."

The matter-of-fact way she spoke stunned me. I stared at this woman with the wild gypsy hair and ready laugh who had knocked the proverbial socks off a hundred men west of the continental divide and had never been fed or feted by anyone but her parents; a woman-child singing to herself as she swam in an ungenerous ocean; someone with no expectations at all.

These were expectations I could meet.

I fell in love at Boston Pizza...

...If this were good classic fiction, the chapter would end here. It isn't, and it won't. Life isn't very tidy...

...We went back to the hotel to dress for the show. There was a message for me at the front desk: Ruth calling to say Dad had died at the end of May. A veteran's funeral had already been held. She'd talked to Beryl, who had our agent's address. I phoned back. Yes, she hoped Dad was with The Lord now, even though he hadn't been truly anointed with the blood of the lamb. Prostate cancer. He had known about it for a couple of years. Shit. That was the reason for his trip to see me; a last visit; the one I avoided because seeing me would be a great disappointment to him.

She said my brother was with her at the end, and had been a source of strength and comfort. I couldn't get hold of Ken, but Fay was at home. She told me that Dad had suffered excruciating pain until Ken browbeat the doctors at the army hospital into giving him morphine along with the aspirin they were prescribing. They were under orders to prevent drug addiction in the armed forces.

We talked a few minutes. When we finished, I put the receiver back on its hook and was gobsmacked with a ray of glory like you sometimes see at the most perfect of sunsets.

My sister.

My brother.

Me.

I am having trouble breathing, and I don't know if my heart is broken or full. I have loved you, all three.

There is language and there are bonds beyond our powers to comprehend. The message had been from my father...

...I told the band what had happened. Like most of us in these situations, they expressed their condolences, tried to gauge how I was taking the news, how they should react, and suggested we cancel the show. I said no. Dad was dead and buried with full military honours. What was between us was forever.

I didn't take the stage that night and play like never before. I wasn't that good a musician. I played as best I could, like usual. But, damn it all, Dad, if I could do one thing in my life over again, I'd stick around to say goodbye.

Later, when the bar closed, after I had wiped the sweat and skin off my guitar and pedal steel and banjo, DJ asked me if I wanted some company for a while.

Yes, I wanted hers.

Western Flyer

Of all noises, I think music is the least disagreeable.
Samuel Johnson

We called ourselves Western Flyer; our days were often sweet and numbered in the thousands. Based in the Slocan and booked out of Calgary we were on the road 46 weeks a year playing country music in funky bars and swank lounges, put up in rundown hotels or view condominiums depending on the contract. It was a good life if you like that sort of thing, and DJ was its soul.

She yodelled like a hooligan Heidi and her brain was a lyric sponge. The downside – if you want to call it that – was that she also sang harmonies to herself through most meals; lullabies to herself at bedtime.

We were a family band. There was nothing edgy or dangerous in our sound or show; our hearts were into folk and bluegrass more than rye and coke. Managers and older crowds loved us while kick-ass audiences could sometimes pose a challenge. One of those challenges took place at the Forest Lawn Hotel during the Calgary Stampede.

The Stampede is to Calgary what Mardi Gras is to New Orleans, except that in Calgary many of the stoned and drunken revelers are on horseback. There is music everywhere and all the time; it's a cash bonanza for the bar bands that get picked to play the big rooms and have no need to sleep for a week.

At that time the Forest Lawn, on the east end of town, had seats for 500 patrons, with barstools and chandeliers for more. It was a rock 'n roll venue that was also a hangout for a big Alberta motorcycle gang called the Ghostriders.

The charming transplanted Englishwoman who was our agent had booked us there to cover for one of her heavy metal bands that had self-immolated at a pit stop on its way from Saskatoon.

"I know you are not truly 'rocky,' but you are versatile," she said. "You can do it. I have faith in you." This meant that she had tried and was unable to get an act that was a better fit, that the situation was desperate, that we were being thrown to the wolves, hung out to dry in the wind.

DJ decided to open our show by singing "Ghostriders in the Sky," a classic Frankie Laine tune from the 40s, and follow with "The Swiss Maid Yodel," an even more arcane hillbilly song that begins with *I miss my Swiss, my Swiss miss misses me.* The girl had jam.

And she rocked the house. Turns out that she had nailed the Ghost Riders' club song, then hit them between the eyeballs with an epiglottal treat so uncool and quirky that their biker hearts turned to mush. I broke into a sweat for a second when a pack of swarthy-looking bearded men with calico bandanas on their heads rushed towards the stage, but they did so only to offer DJ motorcycle rides and to yell that we were under their protection as for as long as there were any of them alive and out on parole.

Other times in other places we would walk hand in hand around tree-lined streets enjoying the sunshine or the rain or the snow. When Tristan wasn't with his dad we would take him on tour along with the kids of the other band members. My brother even got a work visa to tour with us for a while.

DJ had a following of fans and groupies. One real nice guy, a stocky farmer from Black Diamond, Alberta, got her hotel room number and stood outside her door alternating hog calls and marriage proposals until irate sleepless lodgers in adjoining rooms drowned him out by chanting *Marry him or shoot him!*

I had a few fans myself, most of them on parole from mental institutions. A gentle teenaged runaway offered to be my sex slave; I bought her dinner and drove her home; I never wanted to be a slave owner.

DJ and I moved in a bubble of love, and our feelings for each other seemed to be contagious. Sometimes we would play at the St. Louis Hotel on Calgary's rowdy 9th Avenue. The St. Louis didn't provide rooms, so she and I would sleep in the camper in the middle of a public parking lot where the street people hung out. No one ever bothered us.

Ralph Klein, the future premier of Alberta, drank at the St. Louis. He was a newspaper reporter back then. Between sets we would talk about politics and crime. We agreed that they were related topics.

With the collapse of the Second Oil Boom in the 80s Alberta clubs tightened their belts and contracted duos where they had once hired five and six-piece bands for entertainment. Western Flyer became the DJ and Gary show. Duos still made decent money, which we supplemented with more from some minor studio work as backing musicians and occasional cheques from magazine articles I'd write. DJ used her share to buy a small trailer that Beryl let her keep at the Wild Rose to stay in when we were home from the road.

I bought a carvel-planked skiff and converted it into a cabin cruiser that looked like a granny boot. I kept it in Rosebery Bay, a few hundred yards down the hill from DJ's and Beryl's. It was a cold berth in the winter, but my only home after the camper began to crumble. At the end of one tour we drove back from Alberta in a Christmas Eve blizzard that left three feet of fresh snow on the jury-rigged boat dock. The lights were out at the Rose, so DJ headed for her trailer while I waded through the powder and down to the lake where I was startled by the apparition of a baby blue panda, slipped on the icy deck and fell head first into the lake. I slithered out and climbed into the boat's tiny bunk soaking wet. I woke up Christmas morning frozen into my blankets; took ten minutes to pry myself out – just in time to welcome Lil aboard. My daughter had trekked down to bring me a midget Christmas tree in a pot. It had a chubby glass seraphim for its single ornament. I've put the seraphim at the top of every tree I've had since.

Calgary, Okotoks, Whitecourt (the club owner was notorious for hiring two bands for the same gig, keeping the one that would play for less than was contracted, dismiss the other with insincere apologies about the "confusion"in bookings), Rimbey, Alix, Lethbridge, Coleman, Grande Cache, Bonnyville, Red Deer, Slave Lake (the club had a concrete "dance pit" instead of a dance floor; we always felt like we were playing at a swim meet), Drumheller, Hanna, Fort McMurray, Wetaskiwin, Grimshaw, Fox Creek, Peace River, Nelson, Taber, Vauxhall, Lethbridge.

Vegreville, Edson, Nakusp, Enderby (the pub we played at catered to people who never danced or spoke to each other at their tables, but would clap politely until – one by one – they silently pitched head first into their beer and went to sleep), Strathmore, Olds, Innisfail, Sylvan Lake, Revelstoke, Drayton Valley, Bow

Island (DJ ordered a tuna salad at the café; the cook had never made one before, but delivered a huge plate of iceberg lettuce crowned with an entire tin of fish that had been carefully removed from its can and placed upside down in such a way that she could read the imprint of the packing company on her dinner; she laughed and laughed and told the anxious waitress how much she loved it), Castlegar, Salmo, Brooks, High River, High Level, Black Diamond, Hinton, Grand Prairie, Lloydminster, Melfort, Prince Albert, Rosetown, Swift Current... ten years on the road. DJ was getting worn out.

And in my case you could throw in Prince Rupert, Prince George, Tahsis, Merritt, Kamloops, Princeton, Fort Saint John, Fort Langley, Fort Simpson, Quesnel, Hundred Mile House, Vancouver, Vernon, Penticton, Yellowknife, Chilliwack, Williams Lake, Victoria, Banff,...five years stateless, ten years on a wanted list, twenty years on the road. And to think that it all started because of a snowball fight in Missoula, Montana. Well, I'd had a good long run as a B-circuit player. Now my back was seizing up again and it was time to move on.

For posterity I made a list of all the laundromats and hamburger stands in Western Canada. We were ready to settle down.

A Fine Nordic Union

DJ finally let me marry her in 1986, having refused all the proposals I had made before Beryl divorced me. She is old-fashioned that way.

We were married in a civil ceremony in Kaslo on a July day made for bliss. We were given the most wonderful wedding gifts in the world: her whole family attended from Alberta; our witnesses pulled off the highway to make love on their way to the courthouse; the marriage commissioner picked a bridal bouquet from the courthouse garden for DJ in case nobody else had thought to do so; my brother agreed to be Best Man although he held a low opinion of formal marriages; my new stepson Tristan and his friends tied tin cans to our car and Ken drove us around town twice, honking the customary horn; Beryl stood as Matron of Honour, then she and DJ's new stepdaughters threw a surprise reception for us at the Wild Rose; and – to top off the party – Beryl gave us this poem...

A lusty Saskatchewan-bred cowgirl
And Montana white-face Medicine Crow man
Are wedding today.
Wakened from a highland dream
She listens as the drone of bagpipes
Cuts the morning.
Drawing the quilt closer
She sinks deeper into the warm bed
To savor the fragmented images

From her past.
She, turn-of-the-century
In a sweeping straw hat
Soft ragtime sultry summer nights
Punting along a lazy southern river
Trailing fingers behind
Wet patterns that promise each to the other
If they gaze long enough into the water.
There's Celtic in her giggle
And a sailor in he
That sails all night
In fields of mustard and thunder.
Where piney mountains
Roll up alongside prairie sweetgrass
In a little coulee beside the "crick"
He spreads a picnic for two.
A western meadowlark signals
The long slow stately
Wedding procession,
A prehistoric melody
Steeped in their blood and time,
Time to begin.

**Politics
is perhaps the only profession
for which no preparation is thought necessary.**

Robert Louis Stevenson

The Mayor's Tale

The Cowgirl

New Denver

Where did we start?

Oh, yes. The vote was 155 to 152.

Looking at my history, I'd come at it all wrong, but I was a mayor now.

I had received a quite fulsome endorsement from the ratepayers of New Denver: just think of it – more votes than the other guy in a winner-take-all contest with the village's future on the line. This was big stuff and I was not without experience, having served as a councillor since the general election six months ago and the village janitor for a year before that, when DJ and I retired from the road. I had even read the Municipal Act without falling into the narcoleptic coma which that weighty living document to bureaucracy engenders in so many of its readers.

The act and its attendant legislation makes mayors responsible for the "good government" of their towns, then proceeds to only let them do so with the approval of the World Trade Organization, the federal government, the provincial government, their own councils and the electorate. Why not make *those* bodies responsible for good government? Mayors would have more time to ride in parades and lead ribbon-cutting ceremonies if they didn't have to put so much effort into carrying the can for others.

Seriously, though, I was ecstatic.

To the folks of New Denver I was only the latest in a long line of well-meaning citizens who had stepped up to the plate to get peppered with a series of screwballs, flail away to assorted cheers and boos, strike out and rejoin them in the grandstand.

So much fan support; so little time at bat.

Someday someone will explain the nuts and bolts of being a village mayor, and then we can all understand the intricacies of parliamentary procedure, the importance of agenda preparation, the impacts of various property tax classification multiples on both public perception and economic development, the intricacies of municipal, sub-regional and regional financing, how to appear to drink more than we really have at public receptions, the importance of written policy, when to delegate authority, the wisdom of budgeting for replacement as well as project reserves, the need to protect the Municipal Finance Authority from provincial encroachments, and so on.

We could do that right now, but in the end government boils down to its individuals, and I would rather tell you about a cowgirl named Carol Gordon.

She was the village secretary.

She could count accurately.

She liked horses and people, and believed both performed best when kept on a short rein.

She knew her own job and more about her boss' job than *he* did. Like me, she had spent a lot of spare time reading the Municipal Act.

She didn't stash liquor in her desk drawer.

She joked readily, yet didn't give away a single principle.

After my election it took a few months to finagle her boss' retirement without undue embarrassment or the usual buyout bonus, but I did it. Next, I asked Council to hire Carol as our Clerk and Chief Administrative Officer. It was an easy sell and the best single decision the council ever made.

For over twenty years she has never called me anything other than Your Worship, or Mister Mayor if she is feeling informal.

The village pays her for thirty-five hours a week but she always puts in fifty.

We paid for her college courses in public administration. She became a Certified Municipal Clerk, studying at night after she and her husband Kenny finished haying and taking care of their horses. She got so good at her job that village administrators around BC called on her for technical advice when they were in a bind. For a while she was flooded by so many requests for help that I ordered her to cease and desist before she drowned. That was the only time I have ever told her what to do.

We are both fiscal Scrooges, so have been most of our councils. The village went from having under a thousand dollars in a single general reserve to having hundreds of thousands in individually earmarked reserve funds. We keep taxes low and our services basic – but they are some of the best basic services in the west.

When people wanted our rutted streets fixed, Carol worked with the Municipal Finance Authority to float the biggest community bond issue in the MFA's history. It was fully subscribed in a heartbeat.

She worked with our Japanese cultural society to turn the Nikkei Centre from a niche memorial into a Canadian national heritage site.

Carol makes her councils look like they know what they are doing.

We love her.

This is not to say that she doesn't have her downside.

Villages across the Kootenays started hiring cowgirls and cowboys, hoping they were all like her. They weren't, and I got blamed for that. Some of them couldn't even rope a steer, much less provide technical advice to the auditors. There were some mighty messed-up municipalities in these parts before other towns got it through their heads that Carol is one-of-a-kind.

When Kenny can pry her out of the office, she likes going on trail rides. A trail ride consists of mounting a large animal that doesn't want you on its back and making it carry you to places that aren't the barn. I tried to convince her that this was inhumane as well as dangerous. She wouldn't listen because she is mulish.

It was bound to happen: one miserable rainy day in the Monashees, Carol`s horse slipped and threw her onto some rocks; she landed on her head instead of her feet, cracked some vertebrae and other bones, and had to hobble miles to get help. It`s a wonder she wasn`t paralysed.

She was laid up for a while, another injured thrill seeker popping pain killers and swanning around on pillows while council and the rest of the village staff had to hold the fort until she returned to tell us what to do and how to do it.

Cowgirls are a mixed blessing.

The Spike Jones Memorial Orchestra

The time had come for New Denver to write its very own Official Community Plan, a "visioning" document required of every municipality in British Columbia. The village fathers and mothers had avoided adopting an OCP for years, but now the province threatened to cut off our sizeable local government subsidy if we didn't comply.

Public participation in the process is mandatory. *Great!* The final content is not legally binding, but no bylaws can be adopted that are in conflict with it. *Smart!* It is based on the whole community agreeing to the answers to some basic questions. Who are we? *A bunch of wonderful oddballs trapped in a geographically gorgeous appendix.* What are our shared community values? *We all love children when they are asleep.* What do we want to be in twenty years? *Rich and retired.* No, dummy, the question is: What do we want our *town* to be like in twenty years? *Oh, that's easy: small, beautiful, bustling, friendly, mutually supportive but with a good highway to Nelson, where we prefer to shop.*

I was not the person to lead this process.

We took the province up on its offer to pay for a professional consultant to lead the show. Community plans are a dime a dozen, and everything might have gone without a hitch if I had kept my mouth shut and followed the standard procedure that expects elected officials to quietly guide things from behind the scenes. Instead, I convinced our council to let the residents hash this out among themselves in the finest tradition of the New England town-hall meeting. Pure democracy.

All hell broke loose.

It seems that not more than ten New Denverites can agree on anything, and that is only if we belong to the same family or secret cult...Should we replant trees on Main Street? Yes! No! Sure, if they're not in front of my store. No maples! We should plant five, not six, Russian olives because six is one too many...Where is the best place to zone for social housing? Down by the hospital! Up by the bridge! Allow it everywhere! Social housing is for bums; forget it!... What kind of home-based businesses should we allow in residential areas? How about a pedestrian footbridge across Carpenter Creek? Should there be angle parking or parallel parking on the north side of Main? On the south side of Main? In the middle of Main? Let's build a lumber mill! Bring back mining! Let's become a centre for yoga retreats and spiritual detoxification!...The town took to the idea of community planning and ran with it. Soon businesses were being boycotted and neighbours were feuding over issues like whether or not to support Gordon Brookfield's dream of a coloured water fountain on a piece of land across from the Valhalla Pure building.

A few wise souls suggested that it was perhaps time for me to provide some leadership to the process; that everyone in town was certain I had a hidden agenda, and was getting increasingly agitated trying to figure out what it was so that they could fight it tooth and nail as was their civic duty. I stuck to my guns; this was their baby, and I relish constructive pandemonium.

The members of the Wilderness Preservation Society, on the other hand, could be control and conspiracy freaks very similar in attitude to the organizations against whom they pitted themselves. They had been dealing with politicians and industrial corporations for a long time and had stopped believing in open government because they had never encountered it. When some folks brought up the idea of attracting tourists to our downtown businesses by building a public boat dock and amenities at the foot of Main Street, they thought they had discovered my secret plot.

I owned a sailboat (still do) and – before becoming mayor and a part-time liquor vendor – used to charter tours for occasional visitors. The WPS convinced itself that I intended to build a dock at public expense, then use my mayoral clout to cut a deal with the village to lease part of it for a charter operation that would result in the extinction of the kokanee and the ruination of Slocan Lake.

The society's *apparatchik* launched into action with a series of Save the Lake demonstrations, a petition and a call for my removal from office for being a fish-insensitive double-dealing crook. For good measure they also challenged my election on the grounds that I wasn't a Canadian citizen, which I thought was a bit mean-spirited since the head of the society was from Massachusetts.

They based their recall campaign out of their storefront headquarters on Main, where they also sold cedar driftwood and classical opera tapes to help finance their operations. I didn't want to stoop to their level of public discussion but started to worry when no one but Henry, the town gossip and contrarian, wanted to talk with me when I went to the post office for mail. I explained my predicament to DJ, who was fully aware of what was going on.

"Your problem is that you don't behave like a politician, so people think you are a diabolically good one," she said. "But I know better, dear."

While I mulled over the exact meaning of those perfectly nuanced words, she added, "Leave it to me."

A couple of days later a group calling itself the Slocan Society opened a storefront directly across the street from the Wilderness Preservation Society. It, too, had a big picture window fronting the sidewalk, only its was filled with "driftrocks" instead of driftwood and old Spike Jones albums instead of opera. Spike Jones was a talented 50s-era bandleader whose music poked fun at the songs of the day. The Slocan Society, or SS for short, also sold chartreuse t-shirts that said stuff like "You don't have to be mean to be Green" and "I believe in Aliens!" In a polished frame between Spike and the driftrocks was set a copy of my Certificate of Canadian Citizenship, doctored to read that I had the right to be mayor of small villages, but not real cities, as long as I reported to the WPS before going to bed each night.

The SS president and "confounder" was DJ Wright. The other president and "confounder" was one Lorna Obermayer, professor emeritus and wife of Councillor Gordon Brookfield (P. Eng.). Lorna had designed and silk-screened the t-shirts in a single evening, inspired by two cartons of Calona wine.

Seeing the new store made people chuckle when they walked by, and laugh when DJ or Lorna would approach them to sign a petition to Council calling for a ban on ectoplasmic jelly and itchy bras. They got 322 signatures on that thing, if you count the school kids.

The WPS didn't help their own cause by picketing the SS and writing long letters to the *Valley Voice* to bewail the fact that they were being spoofed.

As the town began to appreciate the humour of the situation, the residents regained their usual delicately balanced perspective on me, on them, on the world, and on the importance of completing the Official Community Plan and continuing to receive all those provincial transfer payments.

At a critical public hearing, the community even agreed on a Vision Statement: *New Denver shall strive to become a small, beautiful, bustling, friendly, innovative yet traditional, mutually supportive village with a good highway to Nelson and a preferred population of 714.* I don't know who suggested the *innovative yet traditional* phrase, but we all loved the way it oozed harmonious balderdash. The *preferred population of 714* was arrived at after hours of debate by my totaling the sum of the 58 preferred population numbers put forward for consideration, subtracting the highest and lowest suggestions, dividing the remainder by 56 and – for the fun of it – further subtracting a number of people equal to the village speed limit as expressed in kilometres per hour.

We like our OCP, and since that time it has evolved into a fairly progressive document.

The WPS campaigned door-to-door against me in the next election, thereby assuring my victory. One of its members, a world-famous environmentalist, used to call me regularly around 2 a.m. I always answered the phone in case there was a municipal emergency involving a stray cat or rampaging killer. She would say that I sounded drunk and then hang up. I figured she was under a lot of strain at the time, trying to save the world and all. In truth, she was a dynamo and a worthy counterweight to any oil magnate or Icelandic whaling fleet.

Over time I think the society has come to think of me as a fellow traveler with a repugnant personality, and we quietly help each other whenever our interests coincide.

Meanwhile, thanks to Spike Jones and the Slocan Society, no ectoplasmic jelly has ever entered the village limits. Itchy bras are another matter.

The Queen's Parade

The parade should have gone well. A dozen mayors (all men that term) and their partners (all women that term) met in Kaslo to ride down the main drag, circle back through a side street, then triumphantly ride down the main drag again, as was the custom on Queen Victoria's birthday. Vickie would have been 173 that year, but could not be present in person, having passed away somewhat previously.

Bannered and chauffeured convertibles and pickups were waiting for everybody but DJ and me when we arrived; the organizing committee had unfortunately lost New Denver in all the excitement. Corky Evans, newly elected to the provincial legislature as our riding's MLA, offered to let us ride with him in a vintage white Lincoln Continental. Although we did know a little of each other's history, it was the first time we had met for more than a hello and a howdy.

While we stood around waiting for the parade marshal's call to mount up and ride, I thanked him for sharing the car.

He looked at me quizzically. "Thanks? This car, this job, belongs to the people. Of course you can ride in it." He talked like that all the time.

"You know they put us in parades so people can throw stuff at us," I said. We were sizing each other up, briefly exposing the different foundations of our natures.

"I feel out of place being in a parade unless I'm driving a tractor," he said.

"You have to think of yourself as an emissary from everybody in your riding who'd like to be here right now, but has to barbecue or go golfing instead." I completely agreed with him about parades, but realized the demands of public policy.

We talked some politics; I had the chance to thank him for treating Beryl with such courtesy during the recent election campaign. Beryl, who cared a lot about environmental issues and nothing about government, had – to her lasting credit – thrown her proverbial Tibetan prayer hat and small personal nest egg into the ring to run as the Green Party candidate against him and his New Democrats and a host of others. Without stooping to personal attacks Corky had beaten them all. Without stooping to personal attacks my ever-beloved first wife polled better than some.

Thinking of ever-beloveds reminded me of DJ. Where was she? Like a true First Lady of New Denver she had left Corky and me to visit privately while she went off to pass the time of day with the other mayors' wives, who were awkwardly standing around while their husbands exchanged privileged information with one another. I caught a glimpse of her saying something to the women that made them laugh and cheer. What a trooper! She is very good with people, I thought to myself.

The parade marshal yelled for everyone to climb into their vehicles.

Corky and I hopped into the Lincoln; the mayors bundled into theirs, then looked around in embarrassment. Where were our wives?

They were in a gaggle, DJ in the lead, running down the line of the cavalcade.

"Go on without us!" she shouted. "We're all fine! We'd rather watch the parade than be in it! You don't need us! Have fun!"

A diminutive elderly woman in a ball gown had removed her high heels and was swinging them over her head. I think her husband was the mayor of Grand Forks. "We'll be in the Mariner Lounge if you want to buy us lunch!" she yelled to exuberant feminine laughter.

My wife. *There* is a leader. It had taken her only minutes to end a century-old tradition and strike another crippling blow to the façade of male supremacy. I truly love that woman.

It was a mighty mumchance bunch of political caricatures who had to circle twice through Kaslo, perched like solitary sitting ducks on the back seats of old cars and stiffly clutched trucks, smiling and waving at folks who wouldn't have known them from Adam if it wasn't for their banners. A Kaslo newsletter later decried the absence of the mayor of New Denver, but wondered who the bystander was riding around town with Corky.

Most of the dignitaries – that's what we are called when we ride in a parade – had learned to bring bags of candy for events like this. Tossing sweets gives you something to do with your hands while you scan the crowd for possible assassins. Neither Corky nor I could bring ourselves to do that, but I was toting a canvas bag filled with freshly minted Sandon dollars. Sandon was the famous mining town that is now a ghost town moldering in a gulch halfway between Kaslo and New Denver. This year was the centennial of Sandon's founding, so the Chamber of Commerce had paid a Winnipeg mint to press some beautiful coins for the occasion that were redeemable in trade in New Denver for the whole centenary, after which – much like Sandon itself – they would revert to their true value. Seeing that Corky was ill-at-ease in parades, I asked him to help me perform the sacred public duty with which I had been entrusted.

DJ and the wives gaily clapped and yelled at every circuit we made while our MLA and I pitched fake money off the back of a white Lincoln Continental into the arms and onto the heads of happy bystanders.

"This is grassroots government in action!" I joked.

Corky sighed.

With the Best of Intentions

Before Corky, Howard Dirks was our MLA. He rose to become the provincial Minister of Tourism during Social Credit's last term as the government. His detractors called him The Chicken King because he owned a fried chicken franchise. I love fast food and could appreciate his antecedents more than others did, although I will forever wonder where he picked up his southern drawl.

As his party's poll numbers plummeted, Howard worked like a fiend to bring more money and highways to his riding. I remember him chasing me across a parking lot literally waving a cheque for a New Denver project.

"Here you go. Thought you might need this," he said.

The Socreds were like that.

The highway across the Slocan bluffs needed widening; it was a single-lane bottleneck literally pinned at one point with iron rods to the side of a cliff. It was often blocked by falling rocks and recreational vehicles from the prairies whose drivers refused to go any farther lest they plunge into the lake, but who were equally afraid to back up for a mile to get out of the chute they had entered. When you met an RV quaking at the bluffs, you would give the driver (always an old guy from Saskatchewan or Manitoba) your car and have him follow you while you backed his RV to the turnaround. Along the way you would pass his wife walking alongside the road refusing to ride in *any* vehicle until she was off the bluffs.

Nearly everyone in town wanted to fix their route out of here. Howard did God-knows-what to talk his caucus into approving the project, but they agreed. He even brought the Minister of Highways to a meeting that filled Bosun Hall to the rafters. There were free doughnuts and a giant mockup of how the bluffs would look after twenty million dollars' worth of blasting, widening and resurfacing. Dirks had done it. He had come through big time. The bluffs were a "go."

Except nobody believed him.

"Have the contracts been signed?" someone asked.

He very honestly said no, that was a legal process that would take a few months after the treasury board formally authorized the expenditures.

"Has treasury done that?"

He very honestly said no, and tried to explain that this is how government works: virtually all projects begin as a statement of intent; there was money earmarked in the provincial budget for the job; everything else would follow in due course, but could be changed or halted at any time if there was a problem.

"So all we are really getting from you is a big model, a photo op and empty promises."

The crowd went snaky.

"Shame! Liar! Smoke and mirrors! Never trust a Socred! "

Poor Howard was crucified for telling the complex truth.

Nevertheless he kept his word. The highway was widened and opened to traffic a month before the provincial election. Did he gain any votes with that road? Not from anyone up the lake, because now that it was easy for double-trailer semis to negotiate the bluffs, chip trucks bound for the Castlegar mill began sharing the highway that our residents had figured was going to be for their own private use.

He was unceremoniously dumped by the voters on election day. I suppose you can never be ceremoniously dumped, but there you have it. Corky Evans became our MLA. As a gesture of respect he invited Howard to help him open the Moyie national sternwheeler historic site in Kaslo, a project that Dirks had long supported. That is more respect than most of us will get when, despite our best intentions, things go south.

The Better Housing Society and more than a hundred petitioners wanted our council to provide the village with a community greenhouse. I was never sure of what growing vegetables had to do with housing, but then the society was also calling for money and builders to construct a couple of Haida war canoes for the use of women's groups who wanted to paddle big painted dugouts up and down the lake.

All the funding was going to come from the provincial education ministry, funneled through Lucerne school and the municipal books. Councillor Kevin Murphy thought it was a good idea, so we put him in charge of everything and ran away as fast as we could. Unless you're Kevin, you follow your instincts about some of these "easy" projects. Kevin was a former American draft resister from Pennsylvania and had just returned from a private school in Egypt, which he had left because all his pupils had rich parents and the Internet connections were lousy. He had been raised a Catholic and didn't believe in instincts.

So how long did it take to build a 20' by 30' greenhouse frame with a seasonal vinyl roof?

Two years.

There were ninety-two weeks of meetings with provincial representatives, the school district, the school board, the neighbours (who opposed it if it was going to be near their homes because it might lower the resale value of their property, but favoured it if it was going to be erected near somebody else's place), the Better Housing Society (which supported it completely as long as nobody opposed it, in which case they had grave concerns about the entire thing), Lucerne's principal and teachers (who needed to develop a full curriculum for students using the greenhouse, as well as a maintenance and replacement schedule for same), the Parent Advisory Committee (one mother asked: what in the world does growing food have to do with education?), council, Carol (who doggedly filled postal vans with the required reams of paperwork and saturated the airwaves with the required gigabytes of email), the registered professional engineer who had to review and approve "structures," and the builders themselves.

The actual construction took three months, not a long time when you consider that the building inspector only came to town once a week, one official went on a cruise ship holiday just when he was supposed to sign off on part of the plans, and the local contractor kept leaving to build real houses. A lesser man would have walked away and let somebody else sort things out. Not Kevin. He was on site daily to do what he could. However, he was not a carpenter, so he asked for and received what he thought were the voluntary services of a handyman to finish framing the damned thing.

The handyman didn't remember volunteering, and billed the project $700, which Kevin personally paid.

I could be wrong, but I believe Kevin also agreed to be the community greenhouse keeper and maintenance man until his 80th birthday.

Despite his best intentions, half the village still can't understand why it would take a man so long to do something so easy.

Playing It By Ear

With a couple of exceptions, there is nothing that teaches you how to be a politician; it is too complicated; there are too many variables and the pupil's life expectancy is seen as too short to be worth an investment in education. Contemporary wisdom says that you don't send a pig to school if you intend to butcher it in the autumn.

Career staff can be a fountain of information for elected officials, one which typically runs dry if you think of doing something the staff doesn't want to do. I knew a city administrator who led his mayor to believe he could only vote at meetings to break a tie. The administrator thought the mayor was a bozo and didn't want His Worship's wishes to confuse things more than necessary. When I met him, the mayor was popular with everyone, had been in office for five years and had voted only one time.

From the instant you're elected you are pretty much on your own, a kid holding the keys to an alternate universe. All you have to do is be honest with yourself, keep your eye on the ball, look out, learn fast, play it by ear and make it up as you go along. That means different things to different people.

Back in the 70s a miner named Vandroy Hanson was our mayor. We needed a new water system but were already in debt to the hilt. It was going to cost $700,000 for a water tower, wells, pumps, pipes and line.

So he put on his green and lemon plaid sport coat and his orange tie and headed for Victoria to discuss ways to raise a lot of bucks.

Van was told to unincorporate the mighty engine of progress that was New Denver, leaving it to be no more than a wide spot in the road along Highway 6 instead of British Columbia's oldest patented village. We would lose the right to have a mayor's office (we didn't have one) and a municipal crest (we didn't want one) and town flag (we couldn't agree on the design for one), but as an "unorganized territory" we could ask the regional district to assume responsibility for a loan.

Hanson refused. Not point blank; he simply ignored the directions he was given, and held an iconic television interview on the steps of the legislature that caused a groundswell of public support for the little miner with really awful taste in clothes.

Then he disappeared on a long fishing trip.

He came back with a cooler full of trout to learn that the province had blinked; New Denver would be allowed to exceed its debt limit. Van celebrated by cutting down all the trees on Main Street, so their roots wouldn't interfere with the pipe-laying crew. Out with the old; in with the new.

That's the legend, as I was taught it, of how New Denver came to have the pure, clean water that bubbles from its two deep wells, one of them dug on provincial land. Van forgot to ask permission. I'm sure he felt badly about the oversight.

The province tried to forget the entire affair.

Stuck in hardball negotiations with a crown corporation, provincial cabinet minister The Honourable Corky Evans hired a college co-ed – a political science major – to interrupt him every fifteen minutes or so. She appeared to be speaking directly to the premier on her Bluetooth while she handed Corky important papers to read and sign.

"Who is the girl?" the corporate execs finally asked. They were familiar with his regular staff.

"Oh, she works for the premier. Showed up this morning. 'Spy' is not the word to use, but it looks like he wants us to settle our stuff tonight. You know how he is."

The premier was Glenn Clark, so the execs sat up and took notice. An agreement was reached that evening.

Recalling the day years afterward, Corky told me that he never uttered an untrue word; as far as he was concerned, they were all working for the premier and the people of BC. I asked him if he remembered what the "important papers" were that she brought in for him.

"Yeah, I remember a couple. One of them was a memo asking if I wanted her to order in some sushi."

The formation of the Columbia Basin Trust is a classic story of making it up as you go along.

Back in the days when the USA was carpet-bombing Southeast Asia and experimenting with Agent Orange, British Columbia was building dams. They would be used to control floods and to create reservoirs, maximizing power generation on the American end of the Columbia River. Half the money derived from the increased hydro power would be returned to the province.

It was a good deal for governments and hydroelectric companies on either side of the border – not so good for individuals who owned property that was expropriated for a song in order to create the vast holding tanks that were the reservoirs. Farms, orchards and homesteads in the Regional District of Central Kootenay disappeared beneath the fluctuating waters of the newly-created Lower Arrow Lake; more were similarly lost throughout the Canadian side of the Columbia Basin.

Regional districts are a sort of county government unique to British Columbia. Central Kootenay, which is the size of the state of New Jersey, is run by twenty directors who represent all the region's municipalities and rural areas. They have influence with the province whenever their members can work together.

For 30 years residents of the RDCK justifiably griped about how British Columbia's electrical prosperity had come at their expense. Finally, in the 90s, something wonderful happened when the planets aligned to bring the governing New Democratic Party and Corky together with our district administrator Reid Henderson and a long drink of water with armadillo eyes by the name of Josh Smienk. The result was the creation of the CBT, or more simply the Trust.

With more than $500 million in assets, the Trust is managed by a consortium of local, First Nations and resident provincial directors. It delivers all kinds of social, environmental and economic development programs throughout the basin.

How do you create something like this? Josh and Corky and Reid know the whole story and maybe someday they will share it with us. What I know for certain is that Josh – who was an RDCK director at the time – lived on fast food and the kindness of strangers for nearly two years as he balanced the development of grassroots consensus with the realities of political give-and-take and the pressures of having only one chance to get it right. Corky did the same from the provincial side. Our district seconded Reid to be its liaison with the other local government founding members and to handle the administration of this process, working with lawyers to turn seat-of-the-pants bargaining into the basis of legislation.

Our land is still under water but, thanks to Josh and Corky and Reid and many others, basin residents have a substantial benefit to show for it.

Lone Wolf

Politics is a contact sport. For the most part, successful politics is also the result of a team effort. There are rare exceptions, one of which occurred at the Union of British Columbia Municipalities' annual convention.

The UBCM is local government's official lobby group to the provincial government, and it meets every autumn to hold its business meeting and tell its executive what provincial and federal legislation to call for or fight against in the upcoming year. It's been around for a century, and initiated many good public programs – and a few dumb ones – at the direction of its members.

Every elected councillor, mayor and regional district director in BC can be a UBCM member and gets a vote at the convention.

Upwards of 1500 delegates attend, and you can often find almost a quarter of them attending the policy debates and votes on the floor resolutions.

Another quarter is tied up at the Meat Market, which is my term for the non-stop brief face-to-face meetings you can schedule with overworked cabinet ministers and their staffs. These usually boil down to a special request for more money or ambulances or policemen for your town.

A quarter hang out at the trade fair, where you can enter contests for daily prize draws, talk golf or pick up free pens, mugs, baseball caps, thermoses, plastic heel lifts, day-glow nametags and all kinds of equally necessary stuff while listening to salespeople pitch their wares.

The rest are registered at public expense, but never seen on the convention grounds except at the closing banquet. Some are in bed with the flu; some have been kidnapped and are being held for ransom by activists with close ties to the Canadian Taxpayers' Federation; others are out shopping or spending the week visiting nearby friends and relatives.

A former newspaperman named Bruce Simms was working as a lobbyist for the forest industry. He was tough and had the ear of the UBCM Executive, which was going through a gung-ho pro-industry phase. His mission was to get our association to sign an unprecedented Memorandum of Understanding (politicians capitalize the term to make it seem more important than it is) and – more to the point – lobby for a $30 million provincial ad campaign promoting BC timber, most of which was being shipped out of the country for processing and resale.

A few nobodies like me had questioned the program and the whole idea of formally tying UBCM's independent reputation to the interests of any sector group, but it was a civic election year and forest companies were again, illegally but effectively, being cut out of the American market by our neighbours to the south, so they were getting even more public sympathy than usual. Our words carried no weight, and I guess that is fair, although the way Simms orchestrated the entire process made me mad. Voting on the program was scheduled to take place at an ungodly hour on Friday morning, the last day of the convention.

Earlier in the week a lumber mill in Port Cook had burned to the ground, putting nearly two hundred employees out of work. The owners said that, given the current business climate, they might not rebuild, but of course would keep their logging rights. The fire was the talk of the pro-industry conventioneers who, at their core, were sincere folks elected by their peers to fight for the prosperity of their communities.

Friday morning is the toughest day for delegates, capping a week of meeting, arguing, networking, voting on resolutions they never quite found the time to read beforehand, electing each other to eclectic committees, dining out, pub crawling, shopping, trying to stay awake during seminars on sewerage regulations and attending a stream of corporate open houses. By the way, Corky Evans once showed me how it is possible to make it through an entire convention living on nothing but the canapés and fruit juice supplied at these open houses, thereby freeing up more time for politicking.

On this Friday morning there were only 65 delegates on the floor to vote for the Memo and the money; 65 diehards out of 1500. I had come to register my single vote in opposition, but got another idea when I looked around the floor and saw who was there: mainly councillors and mayors from the Island's mill towns.

We endorsed the Memo by a vote of 65-0. Supporting it galled me, but there was a bigger fish to fry: the tax-supported $30 million ad campaign. Without money, the Memo was nothing more than an unfortunate collection of words, and it's easier to influence a crowd if you are part of it.

The money resolution was duly moved and put to the delegates for discussion. I waited until a couple of men had spoken in favor of it, then went to the microphone.

"Mr. Chairman, I fully agree with the previous speakers (polite cheers). The forest industry is the backbone of BC's economy, and vital to resource communities like yours and mine. That's why we just called for a Memo of Understanding between the forest sector and UBCM (cheers).

"But we have a bigger problem today, Mr. Chair. Everybody here knows about the mill burning down in Port Cook. The mayor and council are right here (I pointed to them), and their people are hurting. The province has told us that it will take our advice on how to spend thirty million to help our industry. Advertising is great – our timber companies need it – but right now the hard-working people of Port Cook need it more! I move to amend the motion so that it will redirect the money in order to get that mill up and running again, and get our loggers and millwrights and truckers back to work again!"

My amendment was seconded and passed to general applause; the mayor and council of Port Cook waved thanks across the empty aisles.

I nodded to Simms, who was turning apoplectic at the press table. Two years of buttonholing and schmoozing had turned to ashes in his hands, all because of a goddamn mill fire and a cheap political trick. I heard that he was canned by the timber conglomerates a few hours later. Business is also a contact sport.

Double Standard

I was working in the liquor store when our two Mounties came through the door. They were jabbering, excited and in the mood to buy some rum, a lot of Crown Royal whiskey, a couple of bottles of vodka, Bombay gin, peppermint schnapps, Kahlua, four bottles of Red Toe wine and three flats of Kokanee beer. They filled a shopping cart with alcohol. A pair of cowboys out on a bender.

"Looks like a party to me," I said, ringing up their purchases.

"You betcha!" said one.

"Just busted a grow op. Time to celebrate!" said the other.

"That'll be $322.75," I said.

"Money well spent!" laughed the older of the pair as he handed me his credit card.

"Do you see anything ironic in all this?" I asked.

"No," they replied.

Going for the Mail

An important part of my job as a village mayor is to walk or bike to the post office to pick up the mail at ten o'clock sharp every weekday. New Denver doesn't have home delivery, so half the town shows up there at ten on the dot because that's when the postmistress and her crew have finished stuffing our boxes with bills and free copies of the latest edition of the *Valley Voice*.

Going for the mail is not an errand to be undertaken lightly. I recommend packing water and at least a light snack to see you there and back.

Yesterday, for example, I left the house at 9:30 and set off for the post office; met Walter Autschbach power-walking down the street with his garbage bag in hand. Walter does two circuits of the village every day as part of his physical fitness regime. He and his wife immigrated from Germany when he retired, and they love the place. As a favour to the community – and because he's tidier than most of us – he decided to pick up litter as he exercised. Our sidewalks and boulevards are immaculate as a result. He's a human vacuum cleaner. We visited for a few minutes.

Along the dyke to the bridge across the creek I bumped into Eunice, who was out for a stroll with her new puppy. She had been losing weight and feeling poorly after the death of her husband, so Doctor Brighton wrote her a prescription for a dog. I do not lie. She had dismissed the very idea but the doctor insisted, eventually buying the little fuzzball himself and giving it to her with strict instructions to feed and pet it and – most importantly – to take it out for frequent walks. It's impossible to pass by an elderly woman being dragged by a leash on a toy spaniel without smiling and saying something. The outings are as good for Eunice as they are for her dog; they both are gaining weight and looking chipper. Doctor Brighton believes that his patients get well faster if he gives them a prescription for something.

Going downtown along this path gave me a chance to inspect the dyke. It is nearly a kilometre long; Corky Evans directed a lot of provincial funding our way so we could completely protect the village. Out of sight to the east there is also a wide firebreak – courtesy of the province and the regional district – across the entire Carpenter Creek canyon and south to Silverton. We're about as protected as you can be from fires and floods.

I crossed the creek, checked the newly installed commercial garbage bins the village had bought for Mountainberry Foods and the Valhalla Inn and arrived in front of the post office at ten.

Henry was waiting for me.

I have come to terms with the old sourpuss. He's like a bizarre relative with whom you know you will be sharing family picnics for your whole life.

"Out slumming again, are we?" he said.

"Hi, Henry. Glad you're feeling well. What am I doing wrong today?"

So he told me. It took around fifteen minutes – about usual. He is a great gauge of how those who dislike me feel: fifteen minutes means that everything is fine. I agreed that the streetlight on the corner of 8th and Bellevue had been on the fritz for way too long, and that it was a shame so-and-so wasn't the mayor. I disagreed that we were expanding the paratransit service just to give my political supporters cheap rides down the valley in order to tend their marijuana grow ops.

I picked up my mail – a single letter – and was standing in the foyer getting ready to open it when a young couple ran in waving their passport application forms. Would I please be their guarantor? Sure thing. Signing passports is one of those rare official acts that pleases everyone involved. I put aside my letter and marked the appropriate boxes that testified I was a mayor/veterinarian/etc. who had known these applicants for a long time and swore they vaguely resembled the accompanying passport photos of what appeared to be two criminals chosen at random from a lineup of international terrorists.

That made me late for a Municipal Emergency Program meeting with Ann and Valerie and Bob at the Apple Tree Sandwich Shop. The Tree serves in lieu of a mayor's office. Rob, the owner, forbids political discussions there, but municipal business is allowed. I love the way my friends so easily distinguish government (good stuff) from politics (bad stuff). To me it's pretty well the same stuff. Today's meeting went smoothly. There were no emergencies, and none planned, so Ann had us do a tabletop exercise to practice our responses to an outbreak of the plague just as an earthquake levels the hospital and buries all the nurses.

That was easy. My role in such an event is to look busy but keep out of the way and sign the backdated paperwork they will give me later. They have everything else covered. They are very good, and in a true emergency the whole town helps out. A while ago a forest fire ran north up the lake towards Red Mountain and Silverton; Ann and the village staff worked with the regional district and the province to run an Emergency Operations Centre; Val and Bob and others found housing for evacuees; the Clear View Club and the Wilderness Preservation Society and the Better Housing Society and Telus and BC Hydro and the RCMP and the volunteer firemen and the search and rescue team – pretty much the entire village – kicked into gear to do their part. Not a single unkind word was exchanged until the fire was under control and everybody again had time on their hands.

I headed home up Main Street, stopping to see how one of our municipal façade improvement projects was shaping up; popped into the newspaper office to talk with Jan and Dan about an article I'd written regarding provincial water standards. Would they dare to print it? Yes.

As I whistled past Jerry Long's, he asked me for a hand to pry a rock out of some ground he wanted to turn into garden. The rock was a diabolically disguised boulder that had become comfortable where it was for the past 3000 years and didn't want to move. We moved 'er, though. Ended up taking three of us and Mel's Bobcat to do it.

I got back to the house at 2 p.m.

There was a phone call waiting on the answering machine. It was from Donna at the post office. Henry had found a letter I left in the foyer. Would I like to come get it?

Don't Flocculate Me, Mama

Or
When is water not water?
Or
Rock Me Baby, safe in the hands
Of science and industry.

A *Valley Voice* Message from Mayor Gary Wright

I recently attended a two-day seminar held as part of the province's review of drinking water standards. Here is what I learned...

...New Denver may soon be without any drinking water. That's right. Read on.

I went into the seminar thinking that very good water comes from our deep, monitored and protected wells...that great water for drinking is distributed through a system modern by provincial standards, and which is tested weekly, flushed and disinfected regularly, and for a quarter century has received cleaner bills of health than most chemically-treated systems in British Columbia – certainly better water than that delivered by the star-crossed chlorine facility in Walkerton, Ontario.

I said this to the panel of medical and industry experts who were there. They straightened me out in no time at all. They told me how all natural water is unsafe to drink and that one of their biggest problems for years has been the public's stubborn belief that under some circumstances you can actually drink the stuff.

Apparently that's balderdash, poppycock and downright dangerous thinking, which they have decided to eliminate once and for all by recommending to the provincial government that the very word "potable" be redefined to automatically mean having been:

- Mechanically filtered and strained;
- Chemically coagulated and scientifically coagulate-separated;
- Polymerized and flocculated (I think this is still illegal in Idaho except between consenting adults);
- Chlorinated; and/or
- Ozonated; and/or
- Treated with ultra-violet light;
- And, after doing all the above, it still must be "residually chlorinated."

That will be real drinking water, they said.

They also said this new standard wouldn't guarantee the water's safety or purity, but it would sure make one helluva regulation. Constant testing and monitoring would, of course, continue.

Since water purveyors like the Village of New Denver are legally bound to deliver "potable" water, we will be forced to meet the above new-age standards. Until we do, the good water we are delivering today won't be legal.

I have drunk some water from the Alberta badlands that I wish had been coagulate-separated, and I have drunk some from west Texas that should have been left hanging to cure for an extra week, but to redefine "drinking water" to mean a filtrated, coagulated, separated, flocculated, ozonated and terminally chlorinated beverage seems to me to be the height of double-talk.

The review panel is made up of sincere medical folks committed to killing germs, sincere industry folks who truly believe that for a great deal of money their companies can solve our problems, and politicians.

Leaving the seminar, I realized that this is one of those times when our best hope for clear thought lies with our politicians.

Just imagine: with enough public support we might be able to protect our good water sources and not have to rely on flocculated sump salvage to quench our thirst.

Write to your MLA c/o the Parliament Building, Victoria, BC V8V 1X4. Ask him or her to keep the definition of "potable water" to that which tests show to be good, clean water.

Redfish

Nadine Raynolds is the founder of the Redfish School of Change. She is about the same age as my daughters, which seems pretty young to me. She lives in New Denver and contracts through a west-coast university to teach an undergraduate summer course aimed at developing the country's next generation of leaders. The curriculum includes a lot of dry reading and a real wet yearly kayak excursion through various terrifying canyons of the mighty Fraser River.

It also includes panel discussions.

She invited me to be a panelist. I got to sit more or less alongside some well-known and dynamic provincial politicians, entrepreneurs, a union president and the head of a national environmental group.

The question of the day was: What makes a leader? Her students were interested in our answers.

Sincerity. Commitment. Charisma. We were off and running. Knowledge. Inspiration. Concern for others. My fellow panelists painted a portrait of God, only with a lifespan and maybe bad hair.

Then it was my turn. What makes a leader?

"Followers," I said.

The panel laughed, but I didn't see lights go on in anyone's eyes. I plunged ahead.

"Leaders are nothing more than dreamers, maniacs or charlatans who have followers. Think about it. Jesus Christ without disciples is just another guy who gets killed for raging against high bank-interest rates. Hitler without Nazis is an

Austrian sidewalk artist who can only wish he was part of a master race. Without stockholders, Jay Gould can't water his shares and become a railroad tycoon. Leaders are only lightning rods for human electricity."

Blank looks. I may have lost my audience with the Jay Gould allusion. Best cut to the chase.

"I agree with my friends here that leaders are people who inspire us and organize us and whom we can blame if things go wrong – but what we truly need is a better generation of followers. We can't all be leaders, but we can all be followers. It's up to us to stop following maniacs and charlatans."

Nadine thanked me for sharing a "unique perspective."

When it came time for the panelists to take questions from the students, there were none for me. Still, I enjoyed following the general drift of everyone else's conversation and can hardly wait for the Redfish School of Change to invite me to speak again someday.

Trees

The West Kootenays lie in a temperate rain belt. Trees grow like weeds here; cedar, hemlock, vine maple, cottonwood, pines, fir, birch and tamarack cover the mountainsides, grow rampant in our unused alleys and would reclaim the village if we let them.

They whisper of beauty in the wind as their roots destroy our septic drain fields and lift the pavement; they shelter our homes from the icy north wind that howls down the lake in winter, occasionally blowing over and onto the recreational vehicles in which we were planning to head south for the season; in springtime they smell of sweet resin, resin that will ruin the paint jobs of our cars; they are home to hundreds of birds, including nesting waterfowl like the wood duck and merganser, but hinder Sabrina Johnson's view of the lake whenever she finds the time to visit us from Alberta. Each October splashes the village with colour as the flame maples and sumac turn red; each November finds our rudimentary storm sewers clogged with dead leaves that the public works crew has to muck out and haul away.

If our residents aren't fighting like cats and dogs about cats and dogs, they are squabbling about trees. Each time I get re-elected I set a new record for incompetence in dealing with this issue, though God only knows successive councils and I have tried.

We have sponsored open houses and information sessions on the subject. They invariably lead to tears, rage or disgust.

We have led public walkabouts, getting public input about what to do with our trees. The public consensus was to tell Council to disregard the comments of anyone who disagreed with them personally.

We have hired professional arborists to identify hazardous trees and place them on a priority list for removal. The list is disputed, amended, reprioritized and disregarded monthly.

We tried to establish a municipal "tree registry" which would identify "heritage trees" and "trees of special significance," but called off the exercise when half the town said that all our trees were especially significant, and the other half said no, they were all a special nuisance.

Volunteers from the Wilderness Preservation Society spent hundreds of hours cautiously pruning our lakefront boulevards in a vain attempt to placate proponents of the Clear View Club, who insisted that there is no point to living on the shore of a lake if you can't see the water.

Through sheer force of personality Councillor Leonard Casley talked the townspeople into letting the public works crew limb the lowest fourteen feet of our mature lakefront trees in order to provide a view without having to cut them down. This compromise might have worked if vandals had not kept sneaking out at night to poison the young growth and ring the old growth. Things could be worse, however. I have noticed that the vandals only target the foliage directly across the street from houses belonging to members of the Clear View Club. Funny coincidence, but that's life.

The Viking

I liked Bengt Olafson, although working with the valley's 260-pound abrasive rural director presented some unique challenges.

He was the only Central Kootenay director who, in twenty years, I saw sworn into office sporting a black eye and a broken nose: the result of a vigorous post-election debate in a parking lot down around Winlaw.

The second generation Swedish Canadian was forever getting sucker-punched by disgruntled constituents in the pubs he insisted we head for to "debrief" after regional district meetings. I was often reluctant to intervene in these situations because he usually deserved some kind of chastisement, but I eventually shouted warnings whenever I saw somebody with a pool cue coming up behind him.

Bengt had been a raving prairie socialist, but something had happened in Saskatchewan that turned him into a raving free-enterpriser in British Columbia. The key to Bengt – as I saw it – was that he was raving in both provinces. He made me laugh, and was a hoot to be around as he mangled the cliques that form within the appointed volunteer groups which manage our fire halls, recreation and parks programs, television relay stations, water systems and economic development programs. I suppose it is only human nature for people who elect and turf their representatives without much reason to go squirrely when those representatives appoint and turf *them* without much reason.

Bengt and I were at a conference in the East Kootenays. At the obligatory evening wine-and-cheese reception he drank a whole lot of wine, skipped the cheese and began exchanging verbal barbs with John Voykin, a gentle-mannered but equally outspoken fellow director. Voykin, a natural and religious pacifist, was at a loss when Bengt was reduced to calling him names and daring him to settle matters like a man, with his fists.

"What do you do with people like that?" Voykin steamed. "I will not speak to him again until he apologizes." This was not good news since the three of us had been working together on some district service legislation; bad blood would kill it.

Unlike my two friends, I had been drinking neither wine nor beer. I had been sipping scotch, and I had learned a few things as a bar musician.

"I'll talk to him, John," I said.

A check with witnesses to their dispute verified John's version of events, so I found Bengt, still at the bar, deep in his cups and spouting his favourite lines from the saga of *Beowulf* to anyone who would listen.

"Bengt, please finish your drink and come with me. We have a problem," I said.

"It's that damned Russian, isn't it?" Voykin was a Doukhobor.

"No. It's that damned Swede," I said.

"Coward. Won't fight. Talks tough, but won't fight," he muttered, following me out into the private dark that ringed the conference centre.

"You have to apologize to him, Bengt."

"No I don't."

"You don't score any points by asking a pacifist to fight."

"Don't care. He pissed me off."

"We all have to work together."

"Says who?" he boomed.

"Me."

"Wanna fight?" he asked.

"Sure. How about right here," I said.

"Right now?" He was befuddled.

"Right now," I said.

"Alright, you asked for it." Bengt turned sideways in the shadows, cocking his right arm for a haymaker.

"There's only one rule," I said.

"Rule? There is no rule in fighting," he snorted.

"I have a rule for this fight. Will you allow me *one*?"

"Yeah, yeah. I can beat you any which way."

"Thanks. Here's the rule, Bengt, so listen close: whoever wins has to apologize to John Voykin for acting like a drunken idiot. Got it?"

There was a pause as my friend let the words soak through the alcohol into the "funny spot" in the brain that appreciates humour. He chortled, then laughed until he got the hiccups.

"Oh, ho ho! You win either way! Oh, ho ho!"

"Or let me beat you up, and *I'll* apologize," I offered.

"Oh, ho ho! That'll (hiccup) never happen! You couldn't beat me in a (hiccup) fair fight. Oh, (hiccup) ho ho!"

Together we unsteadily weaved our way back to my hotel room to finish off my single malt while we shot the breeze and I drafted a written apology that he signed. Being Bengt, he recanted after sobering up, but eventually told Voykin that he was sorry.

A few months later, after the successful passage of the bylaws I was talking about, the Viking allowed himself to be led into another local government reception on a chain attached to a spiked dog collar around his neck. Our directors took turns keeping him obedient. Everyone had a great time.

Tilting at Windmills

The patented municipality of New Denver is overrun with Don Quixotes forever tilting at windmills and Sir Gawains in search of the Holy Grail. I love this place, full of hopeless knights errant.

We have fought with Telus, our phone company, to get broadband transmission into town.

We have fought with them to keep cellphone transmission out of town.

We have fought the incursions of cable TV providers because we prefer the service provided through the regional district by our own volunteers.

We have fought with BC Hydro to prevent our old-fashioned power meters from being replaced with new hi-tech ones that will let somebody in Vancouver know when we're cooking breakfast.

We are always fighting with the Ministry of Education to save our school.

We have fought with the Ministry of Forests to prevent logging in our watershed. Ninety locals were once arrested for blockading the access road to a particular cut block. Beryl was among them. Our RCMP station only has a single detention cell, so the Mounties flagged the lawn beside their office with incident tape and called it a jail. When you were arrested, you had to go to jail and stay inside the tape while people brought you coffee and sandwiches from the Apple Tree. You could leave to use the station's toilet, but you had to come right back. It was a Canadian moment. The logging went ahead and turned out to be the best example of good forestry practices the valley has ever seen, thanks in part to all the fuss we made.

We have fought with the Ministry of Health to save the obstetrics unit at our hospital. When that failed, we fought to save our hospital. When that failed and it was downgraded to the status of a health unit, we fought to save its emergency services.

It was satisfying to lead the charge with Leonard Casley and Bill Roberts. My heart swelled with pride to see my daughters helping to organize the concomitant televised protest march. We won that battle.

When we had a chance to get a million dollars' worth of social housing at the cost of relocating the health unit's helipad, we fought among ourselves. Actually, it was me against almost everybody in the north valley over that debacle. They said: *The helipad was put right where it is for a reason.* I said: *And now there is a reason to move it.* Perhaps it was not one of my best slogans. It's a wonder I wasn't lynched from the nearest cottonwood. The helipad remained precisely where it had been placed thirty years ago. The housing went to Nakusp.

Afterwards, my constituents graciously picked me up, dusted me off and asked me to (1) increase local employment, (2) build a public restroom on Main Street without it costing anybody anything, (3) make us less reliant on processed foods and (4) find someone to open a full-time year-round restaurant.

So I came up with a plan. The village would create its own development company, which would in turn use municipal and grant capital to build a state-of-the-art greenhouse and ecology centre on land we own east of town. The municipal corporation would hire a farm family to grow organic produce. They and more people would live in community housing on the property – rental units paid for with money from senior governments, the Columbia Basin Trust and a co-op housing society. The units would be capitalized over time. Rental income and farm profits would accrue to the credit of the municipality. We would also buy a building on Main Street and turn it into a full-time year-round restaurant (with a public restroom) to be leased to a private party chosen to manage it. It would feature produce from the greenhouse. We wouldn't have to waste any more time holding endless meetings to discuss community gardens and local food sustainability because fresh fruit and vegetables from our own farm would be delivered door-to-door to every house in town by our augmented village crew as they did garbage pick-up. We could spend our summers knocking back tequila Caesars and thinking of other ways to torture Kevin Murphy.

The complete program could be delivered for less municipal taxation than it cost to pave our streets. The prospects gave me goose bumps. They gave everyone else the heebie jeebies.

"Are you demented? That's communism. We want free enterprise," they said.

"You also said you wanted public toilets. Do you want free enterprise toilets?"

"Alright," they replied. "If you're going to quibble and go logical on us, we *really* want communist toilets, free enterprise restaurants, food subsidized by anyone but us, and a municipal plan from you to make it all happen."

Oh well, back to the drawing board.

Meanwhile Corky Evans was tilting at some windmills of his own.

He tried but failed to get the chip trucks off our highway to Nelson.

He tried with slightly more success to settle a century's worth of disputes between our Doukhobor factions and the provincial government.

He won the fight to set up the Basin Trust.

Twice he failed gloriously to wrest control of the government from his own party establishment, running for party leader against Glenn Clark, and later Ujjal Dosangh.

He won the fight to keep tolls off the world's longest free ferry across Kootenay Lake; he even managed to get a bigger new one launched. It's called the *Osprey*, and DJ likes the fact that she can order hot dogs from its galley to eat during the crossing.

He knocked a few planks off the windmill that is the forest industry, forcing it to occasionally share with small outfits some of the public land its elite trades around like poker chips.

During his tenure as Minister of Agriculture he inspired programs to promote the fruit of BC's orchards as The Best in the World in an effort to secure a specialty market in the face of world-wide competition.

He and some of our orchard regions tried and failed to sterilize all the codling moths that make fruit less attractive at the grocery store. It was a grand idea that was supposed to eliminate the need for pesticides. It was as successful as the United Nations' efforts to stem global population growth, only more expensive. You don't win them all.

When Corky learned that I sometimes cut the taxpayers' costs of my business trips to Victoria by sleeping in my car, he would feed and water me at the legislative dining room and let me shave and wash up in the ministerial water closet. It was great: all the perks and none of the responsibilities. Thanks, Conrad.

I like to think that he and I pictured ourselves as public servants above all else, and that's how we got involved in establishing the Galena Trail recreation corridor.

The Canadian Pacific Railway abandoned its long-disused track from Sandon through New Denver and Rosebery to Nakusp, forty miles of roadbed, much of it along the eastern shore of Slocan Lake. Ownership reverted to the Crown. The province retained title to everything except the switching yard and barge pier in Rosebery, which was put up for private sale.

A swack of us formed the Rosebery Parklands Society and raised enough money to buy the property. We saw it as the linchpin of a beautiful rails-to-trails park that would keep the lakeshore in public hands.

The province, which acted on behalf of the Crown, wasn't interested in creating another provincial park, so I asked Corky – who was our MLA then – to convince his government to turn the rest of the line over to the Village of New Denver. By a vote of 3-2 the council had agreed "in principle" to assume responsibility for the trail. It has been my experience that local governments vote "in principle" for popular things while they wait for the dust to settle and they can change their minds.

Corky came through with his end of the deal; even had transfer ceremonies and press releases prepared. That is when Councillor Gordon Brookfield, P.Eng., switched his "yea" vote to a "nay" vote. The village had reneged. At that point Corky could have thrown in the towel, but he didn't. He gave me a month's slack to call in some political chips and convince the regional district to make the route one of *its* parks, which it did. I bet he caught flak in Victoria for jumping the gun that way, but he never teased me or made me do fifty push-ups for not keeping the troops in order. He is not much of a drill instructor.

The Galena Trail is now a fat-tire cyclist's dream, with a bridge and a nifty cable car to help get you across and through Carpenter Creek Canyon, so you can coast down the flank of Goat Mountain to swim in Rosebery Bay.

Ethics and Fine Dining

Grub first, then ethics.
Bertolt Brecht

The regional district's annual convention dinner was sumptuous: great local beer and wines, fresh salads, standing rib roast, planked salmon, garden vegetables, bread from an on-site wood-fired oven, hand-dipped chocolate desserts; a polished duo playing ethereal music in the background. We were in the Selkirk Mountains at a moonlit timbered lodge owned by a heli-ski outfit that "sponsored" the evening, which means the company picked up the tab. Standard business procedure, including the invitation to the company president to make the usual after-dinner remarks and receive our dutiful applause.

Tell a joke. Give 'em one sentence they might remember about how important and successful we are. Introduce a valued local employee. Thank everybody for coming. That's the tried-and-true recipe for sponsors' remarks.

Ignoring custom, the president introduced a slick video that not only told us about his company, but also about how wretched his world and ours would become if we allowed an international competitor to develop the area in ways that hurt his heli-skiing operation.

I quickly sent him a check for the banquet and entertainment; the only one of 150 guests to do so.

He phoned to explain that the evening was meant to be at his company's expense, not mine.

"That's the problem," I said. "I get wined and dined, and then I get your advice on how to vote and do *my* business." If that wasn't bribery, it at least placed me in a conflict of interest, which is illegal for elected people. I told him about a federal government minister who recently had been pilloried in the press for accepting an invitation to a weekend getaway paid for by an international airline. Try as he might – he was a sincere man – he couldn't see the parallel.

"Sorry if I offended you," he said. "I'm just a chopper pilot with a dream. It was only a dinner. Your convention executive didn't have any issues. I've got their letter of thanks in front of me. I'll email you a copy if you want. You people contacted *me* to sponsor the dinner, not the other way around. Besides, how else am I supposed to get your attention?"

Slightly embarrassed, slightly insulted, yet wanting to be polite, I didn't suggest that he write or call our executive body and ask to speak (for free) to us as a delegation or interested party, like anybody in the region can do. My embarrassment came from knowing that we don't seem to have time for all the local groups who want to appear as delegations, yet we're always on the lookout for somebody who will buy us dinner. "Influence peddling" is seen by its pedlars as nothing more than taking that extra little step to make their dreams come true.

I shared my concerns with the convention executive. They checked with a lawyer, who said nobody had done anything wrong. Only one person that I know of who was at the dinner held it against me for questioning our banquet policy. He was a big eater.

In British Columbia it is apparently alright to accept gifts or "considerations" as long as you're in a crowd. Meanwhile I am required to keep track of each unsolicited ballpoint pen and solar pocket gizmo I'm handed so that I can report it publically if their total annual value exceeds $100. The law was passed by provincial legislators in the interest of "transparent government" shortly after one of our premiers was accused of illegally taking cash from a woman representing some offshore investors who wanted to buy some public land in downtown Vancouver. A lawyer said that, too, was alright. I guess the law doesn't apply as strictly to its makers as it does to us local folks. And, by the way, offshore investors bought the heart of the city for three million dollars less than what it cost the people of BC for the environmental cleanup that was a condition of the sale.

A few years later another premier was brought low when a guy from his riding who was applying for a commercial liquor license built him a free extension to his front porch. Nothing criminal was ever proven, but the premier had to resign in considerable disgrace and work in the private sector, where he now makes millions.

About then, I was put into a nearly identical jam by my friend Kamil Aksoylu. He is an electrical engineer who immigrated to Canada from Istanbul and has patched together a career as an electrical contractor. The man is brilliant, but I believe his accent is often detrimental to his business.

DJ and I hired some friends to renovate the little ripsaw Japanese Internment cabin that is our home. Wood ants had digested most of the lean-to kitchen that had been tacked onto the place in the 50s. Kamil upgraded the primitive electrics to meet current code; did it all in a long day; we are now wired to power enough stuff to cause a brownout in town if we fired up all the receptacles he installed. He wouldn't give us a bill for his services.

"Mr. Mayor, it was an honour to bring you and gracious intellectual wife into 21st century," he grinned. "Mayor is poor man, Kamil is rich (he isn't). You are like a brother. Allow me privilege of fixing mayor's very bad wiring. It's Turkish custom." Whenever he wants to hide his natural generosity, his accent thickens, he talks in third person and dredges up his Seljuk roots.

"Mr. Aksoylu, mayor is elected, and you are full of shit." I told him what he already knew full well: unless he billed me, I would have to declare a conflict of interest and remove myself from anything official to do with him, his family, his property or business.

"They don't tell me this when I come to Canada!" he slapped a thigh and laughed. "Kamil must suffer for being ignorant Turk!"

He never did charge us. I put the situation on record, and keep watching for him to apply for a commercial liquor license.

In my experience, smalltown politicians are at least as honest as those who elect them, but that doesn't mean we aren't gullible or easily flattered, especially by big organizations.

You don't have to give us money in paper bags. Remember that we are people who get hired off the street and can be bought without ever knowing we were up for sale. For example, there might be a mayor from the Village of Quumquat, where logging, milling and pulp paper production are economic mainstays. Imagine that he loves to hear the sound of his own voice. He's honest in the conventional sense of that word, but is two bricks short of a load. Forest industry execs realize that he has great potential as an "arm's-length" lobbyist for them. They "help" him organize a Rural Timber Towns' Forum, where mayors and councillors from all the dinky and not-so-dinky villages and towns and cities in the province are invited to "discuss and promote" ways to improve the economic future of their citizens. The forest industry underwrites all the costs, including air travel and accommodations. It will provide "technical expertise" if requested. Lots of press coverage is arranged. The Mayor of Quumquat is a headliner. Think of how flattering it is for the mayors (most of whom live in obscurity and get paid peanuts) to have a chance to join him in "leading a major grassroots initiative" that will save or rejuvenate their communities at no apparent cost to them or their taxpayers.

What are the odds that such a forum will be very popular among the participants? That it will become an anticipated annual event? That the attendees will call loudly for forest industry deregulation, tax breaks, subsidies and increased corporate timber rights to public land? About 100%.

Although they may be legal, the air inside these conclaves is thick and humid and always smells like rotten chicken. I'm proud of the fact that for a generation our village council has held to the principle that if a convention, conference or forum is in our public's interest, we will pay for it with public tax dollars and must be able to justify the costs to the public. If we go to something because we personally support what the sponsor is trying to do, that's fine – but we pay for it out of our own pockets.

Being honest will never convince some people that we are. When the village staff couldn't get another engineer to provide us on short notice with a simple designed drawing for a water system repair, Councillor Gordon Brookfield, P. Eng., volunteered to do it gratis. Henry hit the coffee shops with the story that Gordon was feathering his nest at the taxpayers' expense by getting a secret contract. I wrote an article for the *Valley Voice* and hung out at the post office for an extra couple of hours to explain to everyone that their maligned councillor had done the job for nothing.

"That's not what Henry told us," they said. Disappointment was plain on their faces.

Henry himself was unconvinced. "I know you people. You all lie for each other. If you're telling the truth, show me the paper that says he's not getting paid."

"I can't, Henry. There is no paper. There is no bill. Gordon did it all for free."

"That's what *you* say. What deal did you make *in camera*?"

"None."

"That's what *you* say." It is a favorite expression of his.

"Ask Carol or anybody at the office. They'll tell you the same thing."

"And if they don't, you'll fire them," he said.

"Listen. In BC a mayor can't fire anybody. The most I can do is suspend them from work and recommend to council that they be fired."

"That's what I thought," Henry sneered. He strode off to Nuru's to let his *kaffeeklatsch* know that I had threatened to suspend our CAO if she told anybody the truth about the secret watering-system contract.

Poor Gordon. Politicians joke among themselves that no good deed will ever go unpunished. When my newspaper article was published, it soon found its way into the hands of his engineering association. That august body called him onto the proverbial carpet, held him down and beat the soles of his feet with recycled red Chinese garden hoses for providing free services without their permission. I felt sympathy for him when he crawled back into town and asked if in the future I could be more circumspect when coming to his defense.

The Kettle

John Kettle and his family immigrated to Canada by way of El Paso, Texas, long after he served two tours of duty in Vietnam as a recon sergeant with The Big Red One army division. He had volunteered for the second tour to keep his younger brother from being sent there – the army tried to not send brothers into the same combat zone.

He was elected to the regional district in 2002, and the place hasn't been the same since. Wearing his Tony Lamas and trademark black Stetson cowboy hat, he stomped into his first board meeting.

"Mr. Chairman, who's the low-life who backed into my pickup? Somebody did, and now it's a pile of crap. What, nobody's got the guts to confess? Well, I'm going to figure this out, and when I do, there will be a reckoning." He tipped his Stetson farther back on his head, hooked his thumbs into his belt, leaned back on his chair and grinned at us all.

Nobody had backed into his pickup. It was his wood truck and it was a pile of crap from hard use. He just wanted to make the directors feel nervous and a little guilty before he introduced a resolution which should have stood no chance of being adopted. It passed unanimously.

With our different histories you would think John and I would have hated each other, but we didn't. He intrigued me and I guess he felt the same. I started calling him The Kettle, he referred to me as The Commie.

He was my campaign manager when I got elected Chair of the district, and was himself elected Vice-chair to keep me from straying too far to the left.

He described our respective roles in military terms.

"We are here to free Europe. You're like Eisenhower; you hold the team together," he would say. "I'm like Patton. Keep me from being court-martialled for slapping some chicken-shit enlisted man, and send me in with the tanks when you need to smash the Nazis."

Except for freeing Europe, that's about how I saw our jobs too, and for six years we worked together hand in glove. I kept him from being court-martialled on a number of occasions. He always arrived with the tanks when we needed them. I don't know if we won the war, but Central Kootenay is still standing.

Nobody was better than The Kettle at getting a good seat at upscale restaurants without bothering to make reservations. He would arrive and ask for his table.

"Reservations under what name, sir?" the maître d'hotel would ask.

"Krwselniski," he would say. "It's Polish, so don't ask me to spell it. No one ever gets it right. I only hope your reception clerk wrote it down. The cheap places always foul it up. I'm used to it."

You could see the maître d'hotel's face blanche. He would excuse himself briefly, go into conference with the head waiter, look anxiously at John, then return to escort him to his table.

"I am certain you will enjoy your dinner with us, Mr. Kr(mumblemumble) ski," he would say as John handed him a tip.

It worked every time, but you had to say it like you meant it.

As combative as he could be as a politician, you couldn't have a better friend in need. Creston area Director Tom Mann released himself from the hospital too soon after abdominal surgery, so he could attend to board business; he began bleeding heavily while he was in Nelson. Not waiting to call an ambulance, The Kettle drove him to the local hospital and carried him like a child into the emergency room.

"Help my pardner. He's come unglued," John told the male duty nurse.

"Of course," said the nurse. "You said he is your partner?" The Kettle was always uneasy in Nelson because the town was so liberal that it held Gay Pride parades.

Dropping his voice an octave, the red-faced Kettle replied, "Not my *partner*, my *pardner*."

All in a Day's Work

Tad Mori was a young Japanese-Canadian with tuberculosis when he was forcibly interned here in 1942. He has recovered and stuck around the rest of his life, being friendly and offering help and advice to everyone about everything. He is like the village mascot, so when he calls, I answer, even if it's a Saturday and I am just going out the door in my best business suit for a board meeting in Nelson.

A tree has blown over onto the street in front of his house, he says. Can I do something about it? Sure. He and I buck it up with his chainsaw, toss the logs to one side for the village crew to pick up when they came to work on Monday, and I speed off down the road, picking wood chips out of my clothes all the way to town. I think Tad is 81 this year. I should have called in the crew to do this, but it would have involved a minimum four-hour overtime bill. Sorry, guys...

...Another phone call; sounds official; must be from the office.

Acting on behalf of the Wilderness Preservation Society, Robert Herald has handcuffed himself to an apple tree to keep it from being limbed by our crew. Please resolve the situation quickly so that the guys can start garbage pickup. Kill Robert if it becomes necessary. The office will be flooded with inquiries if the garbage truck is late...

...Will His Worship judge the Children's Garlic Breath contest at this year's Hills Garlicfest? His Worship will be delighted. I truly am. It's flattering to be recognized outside my own bailiwick for my judgement, impartiality and willingness to walk around the festival grounds all day wearing a dunce's hat woven from garlic cloves, bending over with dignity to let small children laugh and blow epic volumes of fume-sodden carbon dioxide up my nose. I greatly prefer it to judging the Adults' Garlic Breath contest...

... I am drenched with spray, sitting on the bow of John Kadz's runabout as he slams south down the lake into the teeth of a summer gale. A few minutes ago I had been visiting with him, sheltered in the marina while he worked on repairs to his spare outboard motor, when our volunteer Search and Rescue team raced down the docks to their boats. A pair of canoeists have capsized off Nemo Creek.

John is not a year-round resident; he's a music professor and cellist from Alberta, but he, too, loves everything about this country. Without a second's thought, he adds his boat – and me – to the rescue flotilla. We all pound towards Nemo, fanning out in a search pattern that will increase the chances of somebody seeing something in this nasty weather.

What I see – as we take a whopping from the water – is John's spare outboard ripping from its clamps at the stern and sailing ten feet into the air behind his head before disappearing into the waves. Adios, fifteen hundred bucks.

John has seen it, too. He yells, "Now I don't have to fix it!"

The search line locates the two paddlers, who have wisely worn lifejackets and stayed with their craft. Nigel, Keith and Leonard reach them first, fish them aboard their bigger boat and secure lashings to tow the canoes. There's nothing more for us to do except carefully slide home without getting swamped on the backs of the breakers.

John doesn't tell anyone about the loss of his motor, so I do. The rescue team quietly raises money to replace it...

...It's Jim Gustafson, the regional district's CAO, with the noon briefing. His job is to advise the board on everything under the sun while overseeing the work of 260 employees and 800 volunteers on our 17 fire departments and volunteer commissions.

Good news or bad, he gives me the day's highlights. Not long ago he was calling to let me know that the RDCK had won a provincial award for excellence in environmental innovation – the innovation lay in getting three regional districts to work together on environmental projects. From concept to signatures Jim had done all the work; the board would get the credit. Jim is very modest.

Today he and I have apparently bought the district a cliff overlooking Rosebery Bay. The agreement we signed with the province was for the wrong parcel of land; we wanted a piece north of there for a new transfer station. A staff mapping error; these things happen.

"How do you want to straighten this out?" I ask.

"It's been taken care of."

And it has. Jim is a professional. If it sounds like the dialog has been lifted from a mafia wiretap, I believe it is because the mafia copies its basic business practices from the civil service...

...Tad Mori again. A cabin cruiser he doesn't recognize (he knows all the local boats and their owners) is tied to the Centennial Park dock by nothing more than a length of clothesline. Nobody seems to be aboard, and there is a storm brewing on the lake. Will I get some rope and help him secure it? Sure, Tad.

I jump aboard and rig spring lines. I am preparing a bow line when a naked man pops through the cabin door, not quite masking a naked woman on the berth behind him.

"What the hell are you doing?" he splutters.

"I am here to save your ship," is all I can say. I look around for Tad to vouch for me. He has suddenly disappeared...

...It is winter, with a skiff of fresh snow on the ground. Betty is at the door with a complaint. Her new Suburban Utility Vehicle has been trapped in her driveway by snow thrown by the village plow as the thoughtless operator ran his machine down her street. This is not the first time he has plowed her in, she adds.

I am curious. Our crew prides itself on its superior public service.

We walk to her house; it's only in the next block. Sure enough, there is a ridge of snow and ice on the edge of the street. I measure it with my thumb. It is four inches deep. A dachshund could walk over this.

"Do you see what I mean?" says Betty.

I look at the SUV. I look at the little pile of snow. I look at her.

"Wait here. I'll fix it for you," I say.

She watches as I jog to my car, a second hand two-wheel-drive mini-something, bring its sewing machine engine to life and pull up to her driveway.

"Stand back," I caution.

With a great deal of show and revving of the engine I drive back and forth over the paltry pile of fluff until it has quite disappeared.

"How's that?" I ask, tongue-in-cheek.

"Better," she says...

...It sounds like a late-night riot going on in the Centennial Park campground, a couple of blocks from my place. I walk into the park, twenty acres of land lit by a pair of streetlights. Dozens of screaming, swearing silhouettes flicker like moths in the shadows. A rifle shot cracks from the campground. And another. I am right: there *is* a riot going on, and I'll bet you I know its epicentre. I run toward the tree planters' campsite where persons unknown had driven a jeep into their sleeping tent two nights previously.

A band of Pakistani immigrants is surrounded by a howling mob of nut cases throwing rocks at them from the darkness. The turbaned crew chief is standing in front of his men's sleeping tent, firing his rifle into the air and shouting for everybody to leave them alone.

"Hi, I'm the mayor. Give me the gun before you shoot somebody, and get your guys inside the tent," I tell him. He doesn't know me from Adam, but he complies. The thick canvas will offer protection and screen him and his men from view.

The Royal Canadian Mounted Police arrives in the person of Corporal Wiens, the only lawman within thirty miles because it is summer and the detachment spends most of its summer on holidays. He spins his patrol car – siren hooting and lights flashing – into the campsite. I holler for everyone to go home. Nobody does. I hand over the rifle before *I* shoot somebody.

Several of the tree planters have been hit by rocks and are bleeding. Wiens has radioed for backup. It will be a while before help arrives, so he takes off his cap and jacket and tells me to put them on.

"Here are the keys to the car," he says. "Take the injured men to the hospital, then drive around the park with your flashers on until the Nakusp unit arrives. I'll watch these guys. That's all we can do right now."

So I impersonate a police officer and later receive a letter of commendation from the RCMP. We eventually get backup, the rowdies get bored, and we all go home.

The story Henry tells everybody at the coffee shops next day is that one of the "Paki punks" made an obscene advance to a local beauty queen as she was walking past their tent; she told her boyfriend; our youngsters rose up in righteous indignation.

Henry doesn't try to explain the damage to Centennial's gardens, washrooms and welcome signs. Hundreds of residents sign a letter of apology to the crew.

To keep bogus violence from happening again, the council votes to contract a caretaker to live on the grounds throughout the camping season. We select Isabel Reitmeier, the village's favourite grandmother, for the job. Helped by her husband Ted, their numerous progeny and – if need be – the entire resources of the village, the RCMP and Reitmeier Logging, we know all will be fine...

...Harry Banks, the promising new district director from Area M is on the line. He needs a hand. He has just fired Glenda, the chairwoman of his advisory planning commission. She is real mad about that and is threatening to take him and the district to court. She's a good person; we've worked together before.

"Harry, you can't fire her," I say. "That's up to the board, not you and me."

"It is?" He is wonderstruck. "I was talking to John Kettle the other day, telling him my problems, and he said that if he didn't want someone on *his* commission, why he'd just kick their ass off. So that's what I did."

"Kettle doesn't even *have* an advisory commission," I say.

"He doesn't? Oh boy." The way he says it makes me laugh so hard I nearly drop the phone.

I ask Harry to get his commissioners together and I drive over a couple of mountain passes to meet with them. I go over the rules with everybody and ask Harry to apologize to Glenda for saying she was fired. He does so very handsomely. Nevertheless I tear a strip off him in front of everyone. I've privately warned him that this is what I must do, and less than what he deserves for listening to The Kettle.

I have also spoken privately with Glenda. She is as much of a firecracker as Banks; both are public-spirited; their fight is personal; she knows that she serves at the pleasure of the board, which in practice means she serves at the pleasure of the local area director; she just wants to go out with some dignity. She deserves that, and that is why I am here.

"Thank you for your apology, Harry," she says. "We all make mistakes. And you should know that you can have my resignation any time you want it."

I praise them both for working with such passion (the commissioners smile) on behalf of their community. Harry accepts Glenda's resignation knowing that she will probably now be his opponent fair and square in the next election.

There is one more call to make – to The Kettle.

"John, what on earth were you thinking when you gave poor Harry that awful advice?"

"I didn't think he'd take it *literally*. Sometimes I exaggerate. Everybody knows you don't just walk around firin' people 'cause you disagree. You're better off to hang 'em."

There Is More to Life

Most of you know that there is more to life than politics. I do too; five or ten years ago I even skipped a waste management meeting and flew with DJ to Nova Scotia to tour Government House, HMCS Sackville, historic Lunenburg and spend a week eating cod cheeks. Village mayors aren't paid a lot, so trips like this are a big deal. Besides, even if I could afford it, I hate to miss a chance to talk about garbage. Our vacations usually consist of telling everyone we're going shopping in Kelowna for a couple of days, then tricking them by staying home with the blinds down.

Once we took separate holidays. DJ and her friend Susan went to England and Wales to visit Susan's relatives and do some rambling. It was a rural excursion. My wife filled a whole journal with breathless stories of farm animals and a gannet sighting, her first train ride to Cornwall, of wearing duckie boots in the rain while they tramped aimlessly around miserable muddy footpaths in the Cotswolds. Who in their right minds would do these things?

I was having a lot more fun with my brother in Spokane, Washington. He had bought us tickets to buzz the city aboard the last operational B-24 bomber in the world. The Liberator was the same plane that DJ's dad had manhandled over the Bay of Bengal and Burma in 1945.

Ken met me at the Eastern Washington University campus, where he had become a major mogul in its food service. I got a quick and modest tour of the operation which feeds thousands of people a day; saw him deal with a psychotic but unarmed female intruder who wandered into his office still looking for The Grateful Dead; then we headed to the municipal airport.

The ancient B-24 took six of us on the flight of a lifetime...no seatbelts...no seats...the ground visible through gaps in the crew deck around the ball turret... big open firing arcs in the fuselage for the waist machine guns (two fellow passengers who I believe had volunteered to join the Air Force in the 50s, but had been rejected, spent most of their air time at these guns pretending to strafe traffic on Sprague Avenue). Ken and I took turns scrambling from the tail gunner's position and forward past these guys, across the bomb bay on the catwalk, then through the nose gear tunnel into the bombardier's perspex bubble.

We were allowed to do about any stupid thing we wanted except climb onto the flight deck. There the *real* crewmen were letting the attractive woman who had sold Ken the tickets try her hand at flying this baby while they considered where to go for supper after they had fixed the oil leak on the starboard number one engine.

I had a horrible time trying to close a little metal door in the nose. I had shoved it open thinking it would give access to the forward gun blister, which it would have if that part of the plane had not been removed sometime in the previous 57 years. There was nothing on the other side of the door except a 150 knot wind. I seem to remember the flight crew yelling something at me until I got it shut again. The pilot must have thought the nose was falling off the plane. Then I sat in the bombardier's seat some more. It was sunny. The air smelled like hot grease and rubber and oil. It was so loud on board that the guys doing the mock strafing lost their voices trying to make machine gun noises that they could hear over the roar of the engines.

Afterwards Ken took me to his and Judy's place. He had been with Judy for a long time since splitting up with Mae. There he made me drink a bottle of my favourite port. No more illegal street drugs for us; we were grown men and had long ago put that childish stuff behind us. So we knocked off a bottle of Wild Turkey bourbon. And maybe something else; I'm not sure. There was food, and Judy was wonderful but had a headache and had to go to bed early. Ken and I talked until four in the morning, when he made me go into the basement with their cats and his state-of-the-art recording stuff and go to sleep in a nice bed Judy had fixed for me so I wouldn't be upstairs where they were.

Before I left, he gave me a copy of a piece he had written to practice condensing history into metaphorical sound bytes. Don't ask me why he did this; he was just like that.

A Precis of the Role of the Catholic Church
In the Weimar Republic –
In Two Stanzas and a Tagline

A priest, a banker, a rabbi and a
Nazi were sitting at a bar. The
Nazi said, "I was promoted
Hauptmann today, and with my extra
Pay I must insist on buying the
First round."
Smiling broadly, the banker pulled
A pistol from his waistcoat and
Shot the rabbi dead. As he calmly
Tucked the gun away the banker
Said, "As you see, Herr Hauptmann,
I believe that privilege is mine."
The priest said nothing.
Ever.

I visited my sister in Idaho on the way home. Life was good in Coeur D'Alene since she had stood up to the college's administrators and confirmed her responsibility to flunk scholarship athletes who not only skipped her classes but also failed her tests. It seems that all three Wright kids have had major run-ins with the American educational system – and not one of us folded.

We got to talking about college graduation ceremonies, and I asked her what they were like from a teacher's perspective.

"It's a proud moment," Fay said, "to watch your babies get baptized."

Then she let me in on a secret: she hadn't attended a full commencement service in years.

"No one really cares if I'm there," she said. "The graduation gowns are heavy and hot, so when we have all lined up to march into commencement, I just say I have to go to the bathroom; I'll join everybody in the bleachers in a minute. Then I go to my office, make some tea and do paperwork for a couple of hours. I always return in time to slip back into the receiving line to give *my* grads a big hug! I'm sure my colleagues know what I'm doing, but they are very understanding."

Ah, the dark underbelly of the collegiate experience.

I may never have learned that if I had been in Cornwall.

Interviews, Speeches and Press Releases

Though we lampoon them for doing so, it is part of a politician's job is to give public speeches and issue press releases. I write most of my own, as do The Kettle and Corky Evans. Theirs are more spontaneous and captivating although they can never remember afterwards what they said. Genius is like that.

While we must package and deliver volumes of standard information about budgets, new construction, future plans and the like, every so often we get to be ourselves, spread our wings and fly. That's when it's great to be alive. My favourite public pronouncements include officially declaring the week of July 32nd to July 38th as Valhallalujah Rangers Week, and advising Henry and his friends – who said they opposed the greening of Main Street because it would make winter snow removal difficult– that our guys were specially trained to steer the plow around trees and small children.

Considering some of the statements I have made to the press on your behalf, I would take this opportunity to thank all of you who keep electing me mayor.

There are times when you need to be serious and blunt. The Japanese Consul General who was invited to the opening of the Nikkei Internment Memorial Centre told the audience that, after fifty years, Canada had "finally done the right thing" by apologizing for its forced relocation of Japanese-Canadians during the Second World War. Following him on the speakers' list, I thanked our government and our village for having the courtesy and sense of morality to apologize for injustices in which they personally had no part. Turning to face the Consul General, I expressed the hope that Japan might one day have the similar moral courage to apologize to Canada for its own WWII war crimes against our civilians then living in the Far East. We didn't shake hands after the ceremony.

Years later a new Consul General, Hideyeki Ito, attended the formal recognition of the Centre as a national historic site and represented his nation with consummate diplomatic grace. I hope I did half as well.

One of the speeches I agonized over the longest was never delivered; I guess the mayor of Castlegar forgot to call me to the podium after asking me as the regional district chair to attend the announcement of a $60 million government subsidy package for the town's major employer, a pulp mill owned that month by German investors. Had I been called on to speak, I would have glossed over the fact that the subsidy came mysteriously hard on the heels of the company's reluctant payment (without the required penalty) of $3 million in municipal back taxes. I would not have asked out loud if a deal like this was what was meant by "free enterprise," something the owners constantly espoused. Or maybe I would have.

Live press interviews are dicey propositions for elected officials. Speaking off the top of your head is a quick way to lose it. I like having a secretary or voice mail to receive the interview request, apologize for my temporary unavailability, take down the particulars and give me a few minutes to think about what I'm going to say when I call back. I will always call back. Televised stuff is harder for me: an old guy now, uncontrolled drooling, foolish grin, thicker glasses with each visit to the optometrist; the medium is the massage; I prefer radio and print.

Despite your best efforts, sporadic shit will still come out of left field. I was in Newfoundland at a conference when I was inundated with calls from the West Coast news outlets asking me what I thought about the stock market scandal involving a cousin of Henry's, a New Denver entrepreneur named Morris. Locals had forked over millions (and I mean millions) of dollars for him to invest on their behalf with "a friend" who had found a "new way" to play the futures market, and was "sharing" his expertise by offering 50% annual returns on all the money Morris could send his way.

What did I have to say? As little as possible.

Had I invested in the scam? No. I didn't add that no one should ever give Morris a dime without taking a dollar for collateral.

Would the collapse of this pyramid scheme – that is all it was – hurt the village investors and affect the local economy? Of course it would hurt the investors. What a stupid question. I was sorry for those who put their trust in such a weak pillar of the community, but – if anything – the financial implosion would *help* the local economy: reduced circumstances would force many of the victims to sell their winter homes in the U.S. and live only in New Denver for the rest of their days on earth, hanging out at the post office with Henry and me, shopping locally because they could no longer afford the gas to leave town.

Morris himself went to ground for a while; never went to jail for doing anything wrong. I've heard that he was sorry about what happened. He is a reminder that many of us are miners at heart: that sometimes you strike the motherlode; sometimes you get the shaft.

When Telus wanted to bring cellphone service to the village, the residents voted against allowing it because the concomitant radiation may be harmful to your health. Radio stations from London, England, to Washington, D.C., called for interviews. It seems that it is getting increasingly funny to question the necessity of being personally wired; the interviewers were all angling for a humorous vignette featuring a silly town with a hick mayor. I tried to dampen some of the mirth in foreign broadcasting booths by saying the story was really about who owned New Denver, the residents and taxpayers or the phone company. And the unfortunate answer from our perspective was: the company. In Canada a licensed telecom outfit can dig up your streets, erect transmission towers with no regard to local bylaws and do whatever it deems necessary to provide its service – whether you want it or not – as long as it meets national standards.

I felt almost sorry for the phone company as we fought this imposition all the way to the federal arbitration board, which reached its foregone conclusion a year later. I don't think Telus wanted to spend a nickel on New Denver but was pressured into it by senior governments because the whole town was simultaneously and illogically demanding *more* harmful broadband energy waves in order to get live video streaming onto everybody's laptops and home computer screens.

American newspapers still follow the lives of both its Vietnam vets and its Sixties' dissidents. The Los Angeles *Times* wanted an update on my "post-American" career. Things were going well, thank you. I said that I loved it here, and was being of some use. When the reporter asked me what Canadian politics are like, I took the liberty of sending her a brief overview of our comparative governments. It was never printed, and I don't know if she enjoyed reading it, but I sure liked writing it:

A Canadian Primer for Yankees

In General. Like the U.S., Canada is governed by corporations who write most federal legislation and give big campaign contributions in exchange for "face time" with politicians. If you can buy enough "face time," it's as good as having your own butler in Parliament – without having to live in Ottawa or sit through a bunch of boring meetings whose outcomes you have already arranged.

The British Parliamentary System. Canada follows the BPS. Like you, nobody here knows what that means because it is not a written code; it's a collection of arcane precedents mostly set by Englishmen centuries ago when gin was very popular. One of them says that our Prime Minister must wear a codpiece on Guy Fawkes Day. Another says that federal elections must be held every five years or whenever a majority of our Members of Parliament (read Congressmen) say they have no confidence in the government by voting against some bill the party in power says is real important. Since nobody ever has much confidence in the government we have lots of elections.

Political Parties. After each federal election any party or group of parties that have a majority in Parliament and can get together for tea with somebody called the Governor General forms the new government. The person who can drink the most tea at that meeting becomes Prime Minister.

Canadians have more viable political parties than monolithic superpowers like you and the Chinese, but a lot less than munchkin lands like Greece.

Philosophically, an American Democrat would probably be a Conservative in Canada; a leftist on your FBI Watch List would be a respected Liberal here; we keep the New Democratic Party in the wings to show us a world where everybody who can afford it pays union dues; the Greens are fervently supported by environmentally-conscious citizens throughout the country until it comes time to vote. The Bloc Quebecois is one of our nation's highest profile parties and at one time had dozens of members in Parliament. Its goal is to make sure that the province of Quebec secedes from Canada, but meanwhile to make full use of the Canadian taxpayer-supported MP's hairstyling salon in the parliamentary basement.

The Prime Minister. Our PMs are like your Presidents except we never bother shooting them. Unlike your Prez, our PM can kick people out of the party or make them sit in the back row of the House of Commons if he gets mad at them.

Senators. Canada has a senate too, but its members are appointed instead of elected. That way we don't have to worry about the wrong kind of people getting into office. Senators are often old friends of the PM. In the U.S. they would be elevated to the Supreme Court, where they could rule against reading in public classrooms or something like that. Our senators are expensive, but innocuous, spending much of each year on vacation in the Caribbean.

The Guv. Canada's Head of State is the Queen of England in the person of the Governor General (the 'Guv'). The Guv is always a nationally respected and photogenic person whose previous position has been outsourced. The Guv must enjoy constantly redecorating the official residence at Rideau Hall and travelling around the world while wearing old military costumes. The Guv's only real job is to get together with the PM every five years or every couple of months and dissolve Parliament, call for elections, then consult the Secret Notes that purportedly tell them how to run the country when they've just dissolved the government.

Historically the country runs better during the periods when it has no government than it ever does when the elections are over and a new one proceeds to once again dash the hopes of the electorate.

Neon

If there be such a thing as true happiness on earth, I enjoy it.
The impetuous transports of my passion are now settled
and mellowed into endearing fondness...
Tobias Smollett

On Slocan Lake

It is a hot day in August, and the sun is past its zenith when I grab a brief-case full of paperwork and whistle down the street through the trees to the marina where I keep *Absaroka*, my little pop-top sloop. I jump into her bright white cockpit, fire up the outboard, cast off from the slip and motor out into the middle of the lake before shutting off the engine. The water is calm. I will have my reading done before the late afternoon catabatics bring wind.

When the sweat starts dripping from my face onto the notes I'm making, I pull off my clothes and cannonball into the cold deep water. Scrambling right back up the stern ladder because the lake is damned cold – and I can't swim anyway – I slap a cap onto my head to keep my scalp from getting sunburned and return refreshed to work.

Later I sprawl against the headsails that are furled and lashed against the foredeck stanchion netting. *Absaroka* drifts below the brilliantly melting glacier while I daydream the years.

The pace of life is easier since I retired from the regional district after twenty years on the Board of Directors. The Kettle is chair now, and by all accounts is doing well for a Texas Democrat trying to adapt to life on another planet. Ann Bunka is the village's new director; Bonnie Greensword – who founded *The Valley Voice* – is her alternate. They are both smart and always loaded for bear. It has been oddly satisfying to vote for my own successors. Replaced by women; there is hope for the world.

I confided in DJ after the last election – my eighth as mayor - that this would be my final term. My back is getting twitchy. The stories of all things must come to an end, or else the universe would be choked with nothing but beginnings and plots that go nowhere. Ann wants to run for mayor; I think she would make a good one.

Corky is retired too, if you call gardening retirement. He and his wife broke up years ago – a cost of politics – but he has met another great woman whose gears mesh with his; he may yet live to be seventy.

The sun rolls around in bright puffs of cloud.

DJ has become a sculptress, shopkeeper and author of a cookbook for men who like meat but will eat vegetables if they're in small portions. *Garden Graces*, her shop on Main Street, prospers in the modest way she intended. She is the volunteer manager of the community gym that our council opened on the grounds of the health centre.

People ask for her advice on almost everything.

Each morning she sits and meditates on a wooden bench behind the chicken coop, an imp's curl dancing on her forehead.

We don't travel much, but Jumbo Jefferson flies from back East to see us every so often, and Marybeth Kittredge came through town three or four summers ago. She is still footloose; keeps in touch with Professor Joe Kerkvliet, who teaches economics at Oregon State University. Marybeth never really found anyone to be her Walkin' One and Only. I heard she lived with Charlie Pontefract for longer than anyone else has, but it didn't work out.

Our parents have passed away, and so has Ken E. Wright. One day my little brother's heart stopped beating, and he was gone like a bird on the wing. I have been in the presence of great souls.

Fay is better than ever. Sis reconnected with her first college sweetheart, who is an environmental lawyer in Olympia. She quit her job in Idaho and moved back to the coast when they got married. They live across town from Frankie, who is now a grandmother and I heard retired as head of Evergreen College's computer science department. I stopped by to say hello when I came down for Fay's wedding. Frankie would only talk to me through her screen door; time doesn't heal all wounds.

The kids survived their tribal childhoods and pose as normal Canadians. Tristan is an electrician and hockey fan in Vancouver. Lil is still in Rosebery after side trips to see Oz at his home in Bali, travel with him in Pakistan and share an escapade in Cambodia, where I think he was buying import goods and delivering medical supplies to anti-government rebels. The latest postcard from Ava was mailed from a small island in the Caribbean; it said she was living near a beach in an outbuilding rented from some guy she met at a bar. Our children.

Beryl has found a wonderful partner. She turned the restaurant over to Lil a while ago; still helps out, but has more time to finish a novel she's been working on. Her folks – Oren and Wanda – are almost ninety now, going strong but with lots of naps. They are driving up for a visit next month. It's always good to see them.

Fish are jumping for mayflies as the sun rolls out of sight behind the mountains that feed Wee Sandy Creek. The sky turns magenta and gold.

Maybe I will write a book too. It won't pretend to be enlightening because I am not enlightened. I hate pompous drivel; much prefer regular drivel. For me the most honest and inspiring books are picaresque, where you get born and then you have a bunch of strange adventures and, if you're lucky, you find your way home in the end.

Smiling at the wonder of it all, I put on jeans, sneakers and an old flannel shirt as the evening breeze rolls south down the lake and I raise sail to stand close-hauled in good air for Rosebery Bay.

DJ has driven up to meet me on the beach by the moorage. In the bushes behind her I catch a glimpse of the mythical blue panda that once followed a lamp down to the river and lives here now. It's a lesser panda – the small breed – and in the failing light you could easily mistake it for a beaver. A Canadian beaver.

I row ashore in the dinghy and, hand in hand, we walk up the hill to the highway where Lil and the neon lights of The Wild Rose are calling everyone to dinner.

Heer taketh the makere of this book his leve…
And if ther be any thyng that displease hem, I preye hem also that they arrette it to the defaute of myn unkonnynge and nat to my wyl, that wolde ful fayn have seyd better if I hadde had konnynge.

Geoffrey Chaucer

That's all, folks…
To the people of New Denver: I've served you the best I could, and it has been the honour of my life to have been your mayor.

Gary Wright

Sketch by DJ Wright